NATIVE ASSETS

THE BLOCKCHAIN BLUEPRINT

A Practical Guide to Crypto In An Impractical Age of Fiat

SAE'VON SPRINGER

FOUNDER + MANAGING PARTNER

Native Assets

Atlanta, Georgia

Published by Native Assets Firm, LLC.
Atlanta, Georgia 30339

Cover & book design by Sae'Von Springer.

Cover photo by Ambrose Chua.

Published 2021

ISBN 978-1-7379900-0-0

eBook ISBN 978-1-7379900-2-4

For You.

From Us.

Much Love.

Peace + Blessings.

Table Of Contents

WELCOME

TO THE TRIBE

A Brief Introduction

As my friend DeMarko says, “Rich Rising!”. In other words, great day, great afternoon & great evening depending on where in this beautiful world you presently find yourself enjoying life. I intuit you are well, blessed & balanced. I am humbled & grateful to be guiding you down the path of blockchain literacy.

Welcome to the tribe.

First off, congratulations for continuing to cultivate your knowledge so that you may consciously engage with digital assets & the fundamental base layers of blockchain technologies underpinning + driving the revolution. Extraordinarily powerful in their capacity to foster change on a scale unheard of since the dawn of computing itself, a new era of economic, creative, social & political freedom is more possible than ever. At the same time, should the collective fail to learn from history’s litany of lessons, these very tools of empowerment may quickly devolve into chains of tyranny + oppression. With such awareness it is of utmost importance to approach digital assets, cryptocurrencies, + the broader field of blockchain technology with intention, respect, & a sense of responsibility.

“Blockchain Blueprint” is the definitive practical, *functional* starter guide to the world of crypto. After reading & *applying* the specialized knowledge contained within, you will be among the top tier of individuals on the planet with regards to your understanding of digital assets & blockchain powered products, applications & services. By no means an exhaustive masterclass nor trite tome, this guide serves as the base foundation upon which true blockchain mastery is built. Understand the concepts laid out here, & you can guarantee you'll be able to consciously navigate & thrive inside of this ever-evolving world of crypto currencies, digital assets & blockchain technologies.

Who Am I + What Is Native Assets?

My name is Sae'Von & I'm the founder + CEO of Native Assets. I also happen to be a pursuer of wholeness, balance, & harmony. Native Assets is a blockchain firm dedicated to helping clients who are intrigued by the possibilities of blockchain & recognize its staying power, yet don't know where to begin or how to best benefit from the tech's vast possibilities. We empower our clients with all the knowledge & tools required to secure their digital assets, preserve their purchasing power & compound their wealth via thoughtful implementation of blockchain products & strategic leveraging of digital asset markets.

For context, it's important to communicate that my successes we're not an overnight occurrence but a result of many years of focus, consistency, & dedication. Suffice it to say I've been to the top of the mountain & to the depths of the valley. I've experienced great victories by doing things the right way, & some significant failures by doing things the wrong way. For the sake of rapport - I'll give you the abbreviated version.

Hustle after hustle, business after business, I was draining myself in pursuit of building wealth. I don't mean getting "rich" but creating *true generation sustaining financial abundance & freedom.* After losing six figures on a deal gone bad, I wasn't just broke, but *broken* - financially, mentally & emotionally. The devastating failure triggered a depressive state that lasted for months as I lost my confidence, my drive & even my girlfriend of over three years. At this point, I recognized something had to change.

Once I climbed out of that abyss of darkness, I resolved to take back control of my life to rebuild something better - something more enduring. Never again would I exhaust myself chasing wealth. What changed? I began spending all my free time researching & studying the history of money, markets & wealth. From Rai Stones to fiat, from the Medici's to the East India Company, from Mansa Musa to the Rothschilds & beyond I searched for the keys to everlasting financial freedom. What did I discover?

Well, one day after months of study & weeks of deep introspection - it all clicked. Money is *optionality*. Money is *energy*. Money is *magnetic*. Money is attracted to people & processes that nurture it, repelling all that squanders or waste it. What else did I learn? **Blockchain technology is fundamentally changing the *nature* of money.**

Was it really so simple?

Perhaps. Regardless, I happened to pay a high price learning how blockchain technology & digital assets factor into the bigger picture of generational wealth creation. Fortunately for you, this book empowers you to skip the suffering & fast track your way towards generating profoundly abundant wealth using the same coveted tactics the world's elite have used for *millennia*.

Consider this your blueprint.

DISCLAIMER

Stellar results are not typical. Why? Most people don't take action. In fact, many will read this book thoroughly enthused & intrigued, devouring the "content" - yet won't do anything. Don't be one of many. Be one of few.

DISCLAIMER 2

(Oh, yea. Legal felt quite strongly I add one more)

Any & all materials released by Native Assets (including this book) are designed for educational use only. Nothing conveyed or communicated in this text, by the firm, nor any of it's representatives should be misconstrued as investment, financial, tax, legal or other professional advice as ***we are not certified financial advisors****.*

What we offer is an exploration of blockchain technologies, cryptocurrencies & digital assets presented at the highest quality, optimized for coherence & actionability. While we have the utmost confidence that you will obtain a deep & robust understanding of blockchain tech & the broader digital asset markets that will position you for success within the space - ***we make no guarantees of any results or outcomes****. If action is taken as a result of considering any views or opinions held by the Native Assets, it is plainly expressed that said action is done through free will and individual volition, not by any specific inducement made by the firm.*

What's The Mission?

I want to answer the question - "What's the purpose of '*Blueprint*'? Why does it exist?"

Honestly?

Too many people are drawn into blockchain & crypto simply because it's trending amongst internet "influencers" or because they hear about the life-enhancing money many have made investing into various coins & tokens.

The problem?

Fears of missing out (FOMO) or more general fears, uncertainties & doubts (FUD) have poisoned the mentalities of many, leaving them jaded, bitter, & financially distressed. The desperation for immediate riches blinds those who, if only they had eyes to see, would realize that if they took a moment to understand the industry & it's powerful applications, they could create stable, predictable, abundant methods of growing their wealth – even without risking their capital, not to mention a bevy of other potent blockchain use cases.

Recognizing the massive chasm of knowledge in the sector, "*Blueprint*" was created to provide education & clarity on the value, tech, uses, possibilities, & challenges associated with blockchain technologies. My singular mission is helping you understand how to best navigate the quickening digital asset evolution to elevate the quality of your life by consciously integrating specialized tools, strategies & solutions powered by blockchain & digital asset markets. Whether the masses want to accept or acknowledge it, blockchain technology is becoming integrated into *every* aspect of modern society. In this dawning era the blockchain literate will thrive, while the blockchain illiterate struggle.

So, who is "*Blockchain Blueprint*" really for? To be frank, it's for everybody. (My publisher insists that's a horrible marketing angle - but it's true!) For easy reading, let's go ahead & bullet point this "catch-all" target demo. **"*Blueprint*" is the answer if you**...

- Hope to learn **how to invest** in digital assets for the long term
- Feel excited about **the technology** & **innovation** in the blockchain & digital asset sector
- Have concerns about **inflation**
- Are **tired of the banking system**
- Want to **trade or speculate** on crypto
- Seek **work in the blockchain industry**
- Strive to build **passive income streams**
- Need access to **credit** & **financing** tools
- Sense you should be learning & **adapting** for the **future**

- Doubt the **value** & **utility** of blockchain & digital assets or are otherwise skeptical

The data, intel, insights, information, tips, tactics & strategies laid forth in this blueprint are likely a pivotal key for making abundant changes in your life. But will it matter? Unless & until you apply this knowledge in the field for your own betterment & growth - what's the point? Unless you have an incredible affection for what some dub "Theoryland", you're here for a tangible transformation. So long as you ***act*** upon the information inside of this book, **expect the following outcomes**:

- Confidence about making **informed investment decisions** within the blockchain & digital asset space.
- **Understanding** of **blockchain** tech & **digital assets** at a **high-level** executive view & a **low level** - the specifics, the nitty gritty.
- Securely custody your own **private keys** & learn how to **become your own bank**.
- Create **passive income** streams via various methods like lending & staking.
- Comfortably & easily operate **decentralized protocols** like **Uniswap** & leverage decentralized **stable coins** such as DAI to **minimize tax burdens** & **access credit**.
- Distinguish yourself as a **competitive candidate** for a job or role within the blockchain industry.

Tips For Success

Be Present Remain focused & dialed in as you move through this blueprint. Dedicate consistent time within your schedule to review the material within until things click.

Take Your Time There's no need to rush. There's no need to sprint. Take as much time as you need. Nevertheless, I encourage you to set a reasonable pace for yourself & commit to working through this entire blueprint.

Eliminate Distractions Put your phone on do not disturb mode (or cut it off all together). You may need to put some earplugs in, put some headphones on, or go to a quiet place where you're not going to be bothered so you can really dial in to the materials.

Keep An Open Mind This emerging technology is as novel as JavaScript in the '90s & iTunes in the 2000s. Some could say it's as revolutionary as Ada Lovelace's Analytical Machine algorithm. Much of what you will learn has never been possible before because of prior technological limitations & bottlenecks. As such, you may feel disoriented by all the insights you'll have. The material covered may even elicit visceral responses from you. Some may be emotional responses such as "I'm afraid about what may happen". Some may be logical responses like "Oh, that seems too good to be true! How is that possible?".

Keep an open mind & audit your own reactions to avoid creating limiting biases.

Take Notes Taking notes *at all* is better than *not* taking notes at all (or is it?). Either way, I suggest you write these down - *by hand*. Sure, in certain situations it may be less convenient, but there's plenty of data that demonstrates the connections made between the synapses of your brain are more numerous & more robust when done manually. In short - the neuroplasticity effect is greater when you are writing notes *by hand.* At *least* use a highlighter if you can.

Take Action Convert the theory into practice. Once you feel comfortable with the baseline understanding - give things a try. Follow along as we broach new concepts & techniques so that you aren't just learning, but building & developing a new set of powerful, valuable skills.

Be Uncomfortable Understand you're likely to be uncomfortable at some point - which is good! Being uncomfortable is a sign you're pushing the bounds of your own limitations & understanding. Thus, you become even more limitless.

Be Patient This blueprint condenses years of information into a few hours of reading (& doing). Be patient with yourself.

Be Responsible To take full action on these concepts requires you to have skin in the game - *financial skin.* As with any investment or opportunity involving potential upside, there is potential downside. **DO NOT** invest more than you'd be comfortable losing. (Read that a few dozen times) Be realistic with what you are *comfortably* able to invest. No matter what, always be responsible with what you choose to do with your finances.

Be Excited You have taken a tremendous leap by committing yourself to achieving blockchain literacy. For the sake of perspective, recognize that less than 1% of all of humanity on planet Earth right now even *use* blockchain tech or digital assets. Of that >1%, many of those people are purely speculators. By working through this blueprint & taking action on the information herein you're perfectly positioned to successfully navigate & flourish in the digital asset era. That's an incredible thing to be excited about. So, the question that remains - are you ready to begin? If so, let me thank you one more time for trusting Native Assets to help assist you along this journey towards blockchain literacy.

Let's get to it!

BLOCKCHAIN 101: COVERING THE BASICS

Bitcoin: The Original Crypto

Although Bitcoin was not the first idea of a cryptographically based digital currency, it's the first ever to gain real traction. Some see it as the single key to a more abundant future, espousing it's philosophical & humanitarian heft as the world's premier "nonviolent" money. Others appreciate its borderless properties, hoping it will kick-off a global revolution by stripping the banking hegemons of their totalitarian power. To be frank, the implications are vast & given enough time, all of this could very well come to pass in some form or another. Nevertheless, the core value of Bitcoin centers around the qualities detailed below.

Peer-To-Peer: *Decentralized*

Bitcoin was designed to be an entirely peer-to-peer network. From the miner-driven minting process all the way to private key self-custody, Bitcoin eliminates the need for centralized counterparties + trusted intermediaries. A true bearer asset in digital form.

Though a non-issue for most, dealing with a third party comes with the inherent risk of trusting they will behave in a manner that is aligned with whatever was agreed upon prior to entering the contract or working agreement.

For example, if you have money deposited inside of your bank account, you are in a binding agreement with the custodian (the counterparty) holding the funds. You must now trust that the bank will honor all previously agreed upon terms, including your right to access any deposited funds. Usually, this all works out in amicable fashion. But what if one day things change? What recourse would you have?

Blockchain Based: *An Immutable Ledger*

Triple-entry accounting was made popular by Bitcoin's blockchain structure. Permanent + chronological in nature, the Bitcoin blockchain serves as a perfect, objective + open record of all transactions & users. A fully auditable & inclusive financial system available for the world. Why trust when you can verify?

For instance, let's say there is a baker with an investor funding their burgeoning business. In order to manipulate the perception of the true state of the bakery's financials the baker could hide certain transactions from the accounting ledger shared with their investor. Such deceit is not possible with triple entry accounting because all parties see every single transaction: credits, debits, account addresses, etc., all immediately reflected in the ledger of all the participants involved in the transaction.

Digitally Native Value: *Hard Money*

When Bitcoin debuted there was a bit of pushback as far as what it meant for something to be "digitally native". How could the internet's latest creation be any different from people using debit cards, wired transactions, PayPal and mechanisms of a similar nature. Unfortunately, lack of proper education means most people completely misunderstand how traditional "digital" payment systems operate.

When using platforms like CashApp, PayPal, or even something like Zelle, it only *appears* as if money is being sent back & forth in real-time. What's happening on the back end involves massive global entities like the Bank of International Settlements (BIS) & their member institutions debiting + crediting their balance sheets between each other. Sure, this may be *functional* for the time being, but its substantially different from an asset that only exists in digital space, can't be deleted or created with the stroke of a computer key, and settles within seconds of the transaction taking place, and for little to no cost. With Bitcoin it's entirely possible to transfer billions of dollars directly to someone across the planet in seconds while paying less than $1 in fees.

The confusion so far has been understandable. Modern history lacks context for a programmatically scarce asset with goals of disrupting the monetary system. Though many variants of money + currency have been trialed throughout time, fiat has an impressive track record of eventually crashing to zero! In contrast to baseless fiat, principles of hard + sound money are coded within Bitcoin's DNA. In a world of endless money printing + inflating fiat, Bitcoin seems to be doing alright.

Ethereum: The Smart Contract Standard

A "cryptographic box" primed to dispense its contents should certain conditions be met - Nick Szabo dubbed Ethereum "A virtual vending machine". As the original blockchain based upon a Turing complete programming language Ethereum has amassed a staggering variety of developers & founders building out applications & services never before possible. From the NFT revolution to decentralized finance & programmable money, smart contract enabled dApps are rapidly cementing the foundation of the Web3 future.

Smart Contracts: *Digital Vending Machines*

Ethereum was designed as a platform to create code based digital agreements known as "Smart Contracts". You can conceive of these as blockchain-based "If, then" statements existing as Ethereum accounts capable of holding a balance and executing transactions once certain parameters are met.

Smart contracts are automatically executed, composable, accessible to anyone *without* needing to grant permissions, & can even be fed "real world" data by integrating oracles like Chainlink. By combining the trustless nature of permissionless blockchains with the flexibility of Turing complete code, developers are empowered to create novel apps with unique use cases.

Token Systems: *Blockchain Native Assets*

It is through Ethereum's tokenization process that any conceivable asset, be it tactile or abstract, is bestowed a digital, blockchain-native format as a "token". Historically, developers & founders of projects typically create a token for their product or service as a source of crowdfunding, mindfully building in different use cases to for added value. The initial coin offering (ICO) boom of 2017 leveraged the ERC-20 standard as a wave of "alternative coins" flooded the market, while the NFT craze of 2021 mainly relied upon the ERC-721 standard. To clarify though, not all tokens are "tokens". Technically, NFTs are tokenized versions of other assets, digitally native or otherwise, such as land deeds, business invoices, medical records, Banksy artwork or something else rooted in the physical world.

Decentralized Apps: *Web3.0*

Most internet-based apps & services host their code on private, centralized servers. In contrast, Ethereum-based decentralized applications, known as "dApps" run backend code on decentralized peer-to-peer networks. As a benefit of this design DApps benefit from zero downtime, immutable + verifiable data, full auditability, and private, permissionless access. As with APIs, these specialized programs are composable & interoperable. By combining the power of smart contracts with user facing front ends allowing for easy & intuitive interaction, rapid iteration and innovation has become the norm. For reference, MetaMask, Uniswap, Aave & Compound, some of the most prominent dApps in the Ethereum ecosystem, are all a consequence of Ethereum's "Lego" like nature. Though this new era of programming is still in its formative stage, dApps will serve as the new de facto standard for internet-native applications, products & services in the Web3 future.

Understanding Digital Assets: Coins vs Tokens

Not all cryptos are the same. In the world of digital assets there are *coins* and there are *tokens*. Even though they're often referred to by the catch-all term "cryptocurrencies", it's far more accurate to refer to them as "digital assets" simply because the *vast* majority aren't currencies at all, but rather *tokens*.

What's the difference? Coins are native to their own blockchain, whereas tokens are chain flexible. For example, BTC & ETH are the native coins for the Bitcoin & Ethereum blockchains, respectively. Digital assets such as Decentraland's MANA or Compound's COMP were originally designed to work on top of the Ethereum blockchain as ERC-20 tokens but have since been developed to work on top of other blockchains too, demonstrating their chain flexibility.

Legal Clarity

An important distinction between coins & tokens is how they are viewed & classified by regulators. Coins typically have far greater legal clarity when compared against tokens, which often exist in a murky state of ambiguity, particularly when using a framework like the Howey Test to assess whether an asset should be considered a security. Though the Howey Test is a bit beyond this scope of conversation, I encourage you to visit the *Crypto Rating Council*'s website. Composed of several industry titans, the CRC is an organization that audits digital assets, assigning a risk rating based on the likelihood of that asset being deemed a security. The site only covers a sliver of the digital assets that exist, but it's a great resource all the same.

Use Cases

Digital assets have a variety of use cases. Tokens are typically used to grant special access, signal status or to provide perks. Point in case - take Decentraland's MANA token. If you want to access commerce markets within the Metaverse (Decentralands's digital universe) to buy virtual items, art or even virtual real estate, you must use MANA. Coins on the other hand are typically used to store value (like BTC), transfer value (such as stable*coins* like USDC & DAI) or to pay for fees (like ETH for gas).

The Power of Private Keys

Private key ownership is one of the most unique & important aspects of digital assets. In short – a private key is a cryptographic proof of ownership that cannot be forged & allows the holder (owner) to deposit, withdraw, spend, send, & transfer their assets *whenever* they want, with *whomever* they want, enabling total transaction freedom.

In essence, you have two keys associated with every digital asset - the *public* key & the *private* key. Your private key is the alpha-numeric string that appears whenever you initiate a "withdraw" transaction, while your public key is the alpha-numeric string appearing whenever you initiate a "deposit" transaction. Though the format can vary between blockchains, all keys exist as a seemingly random mix of numbers & letters, often being paired alongside a QR code for easy use. Asymmetric cryptography ensures that while public keys can be derived from private keys, private keys cannot be extrapolated from public keys, hence why you ***never*** share your private keys as these allow for funds to be withdrawn from your account. If you or someone else needs to make a deposit to your address, ***only*** share your public key.

So how do you know if you control your keys? Thankfully, it's a shockingly simple process. **So long as you can withdraw your assets from the exchange or broker you purchased them from, you control the private keys.**

To be absolutely clear - if you don't control your private keys what you hold is no more than an I.O.U. that's unlikely to be redeemable for the underlying asset. If you only care about fiat-denominated gains, no problem! However, if you're seeking exposure to digital assets like Bitcoin because of its inherent economic & monetary properties - make certain you control the private keys.

The Antidote To Financial Censorship

In Q3 of 2021 the popular subscription site OnlyFans found itself in a quandary: ban all sexually explicit creators or risk losing its existing banking partners. This is a perfect example of a phenomena known as financial censorship.

Though they eventually reversed their initial decision to ban the bedrock of their user base, they could (& still should) have integrated digital asset payments directly into their platform. Unlike electronic bank payments, digitally native assets allow you to withdraw, deposit, & transact with anybody at any time- 365/24/7, with one small caveat: you must control the private keys.

With traditional electronic funds users *never* directly own nor custody funds as they are restricted to withdrawing/depositing or otherwise transferring funds based on their bank, broker or custodian's specific schedule, policies & regulations.

This degree of control means at any moment, for any reason, the bank could block your payment, freeze or even close your account & confiscate all remaining funds. I won't go too deep into explaining this fatally flawed system here but suffice it to say it has a lot to do with the international banking system that sprung to life following the Bretton Woods Agreement. If you would like to know more about the history of the Bank of International Settlements, World Bank, International Monetary Fund & their roles in the global banking machine, be sure to check out our on-demand seminar program "*Blockchain Foundations: The Blueprint To Blockchain Investing*" now available online at www.nativeassets.co/foundations.

Counterparty Risk

In layman's terms, the removal of counterparty risk eliminates any need to trust outside entities with your assets. So long as you control the private keys you are the sole bearer in fact regarding those funds. Such clear, unequivocal ownership & control is in stark contrast to the traditional banking system based on the fractional reserve lending scheme. If you're unfamiliar with the process, I'll elaborate.

Fractional reserve lending allows banks to monetize the debt they create when they take the bulk of deposited funds entrusted to them by account holders & loan it out to other customers by abstracting the whole process in the form of various financial instruments. The term "fractional reserve" alludes to the fact that banks only maintain a "fraction" of account holder's funds at any given time - the rest of the money remains unavailable because it's already been given to someone else. For example, if you were to deposit $1,000 the bank ~~is~~ ***was*** only legally required to hold 10% of your funds in reserve, the remaining 90% being leveraged into products like loans as a means of creating + monetizing newly issued debt.

The system was already bad enough, but on March 15, 2020, the Fed (a private, non-governmental entity) removed the fractional reserve requirement altogether. As it stands at press time, ***US banks aren't required to hold any of your money on hand. Not a damn dime.*** In the event everybody decided to go to the bank at one time to withdraw their money - guess what? The bank won't have enough. I don't mean the banks wouldn't have enough cash on hand. Obviously, banks only hold so much paper currency at a time, hence the regularly scheduled Loomis deliveries. I mean from an accounting standpoint, assessing total available reserves on the books, accounts, etc., the banks would not have enough money to fulfill everyone's withdrawal request - not even via digital transfer.

Moral of the story? Hold your own private keys & eliminate the need for "trusted" third parties if you want to be in total control of your funds.

Institutional Opportunities

There are many instruments, products + services readily accessible in via blockchain protocol that remain barred off behind a $5 million wall of accredited investor status within the traditional financial system. For example, you can send $10,000 worth of DAI over to Aave, obtain an over collateralized loan that's instantly approved + dispersed directly to your wallet, invest a portion of that loan into a yield protocol earning double digit APY, stake another portion to earn rewards in the form of your favorite platform's newly released native token before it gets listed to major exchanges + surges in appreciation, & use the remaining capital to provide liquidity on an emerging DEX to earn a portion of all the trading fees as a market maker. This &

so much more is possible as long as you control your private keys. All you need is a self-custody wallet.

Self-Custody Solutions

Direct ownership + direct access are core tenets of crypto + blockchain, hence the popular "Not your keys, not your funds!" meme. There are two types of self-custody wallets you should be familiar with: digital, software-based "hot" wallets, & hardware based "cold storage" wallets. Though exact features may differ, all wallets allow users to create multiple accounts, each account having its own unique address.

Software Wallets

Hot Wallets Software wallets come in two main flavors: browser-based extensions + mobile /desktop apps. Browser-based wallets are needed to connect to dApps + other Web3 platforms, while mobile wallets are best for transacting on the go & convenient storage of less common/low market cap assets. Desktop wallets function much like mobile wallets, sans the portability.

MetaMask is by far the most popular browser-based wallet in terms of monthly active users, but there are many other great choices. Since the majority of dApps only support a few wallets, you may find yourself needing to use a different one to access a specific platform. Raydium for instance, a Solana-based DEX, launched with Phantom compatibility but not MetaMask. No matter which route you go I'd recommend using something that allows you to quickly + seamlessly switch blockchain networks + provides the option to connect a hardware wallet as an additional authentication requirement to boost overall security. As far as desktop + mobile wallets go, Exodus is one of the best on the market with its stunning UI, intuitive UX, & excellent portfolio tracking features.

The main downside to software wallets is their "hot' nature as all funds lie vulnerable to potential hack or exploit due to the internet native nature of the wallet itself. Theft is unlikely given the seed phrase + passwords needed to access accounts, but if something happened to the backend server linking all the private keys to your assets, its unsure the outcome. Though I've never heard of any software wallet losing funds, it's prudent to understand potential attack vectors. Cold storage eliminates this risk by storing all the keys directly on the device itself, not on an internet-dependent server, only interacting with the internet when broadcasting or receiving a transaction. Otherwise, all funds are chilling on the hardware, literally.

Unlike their hardware counterparts, new software wallets are constantly being released + improved with no singular winner. Find something that provides a clear set of features that allow you to do everything you need. Listed below are some tried-and-true options to begin with.

<u>Browser-based Wallets</u>

- MetaMask
- Wallet Connect
- Portis
- Coinbase Wallet

<u>Desktop/Mobile Wallets</u>

- Exodus
- MyEtherWallet
- Atomic Wallet
- Trust Wallet

Hardware Wallets

Cold Storage Adding an air-gapped layer of protection to your funds, security is the killer feature of cold storage wallets. Once you disconnect the device from your computer there's no way anybody can access the stored funds without having the physical hardware key itself.

My top recommendation for cold storage is the Ledger Nano S. With simple two-button operation, deep Web3 integration & a straightforward software app Ledger Live, it has everything you'll need. While the premium "X" model has more memory to manage different assets, a sleeker design & iOS support, having Bluetooth functionality means its technically more vulnerable to wireless exploits than the S. Regardless of the model, Ledger wallets use a closed, proprietary software instead of an open-source alternative. For those wanting a more transparent + open-source option, check out the ColdCard & Trezor wallets.

Digital Asset Transactions

Before you can use any of the available wallets on the market (hot *or* cold), control your private keys or take advantage of the numerous products & services unique to the sector, you'll need to get acclimated with the process of sending & receiving digital assets. Though it may seem daunting, confusing, or overly technical at first - I assure you it's simple & easy once you've gotten a few reps under your belt.

Withdrawals & Deposits

As with traditional banks, digital assets rely upon withdrawals & deposits to facilitate transactions, (i.e., to use your digital assets). Once you understand the mechanics & are comfortable with the transaction process, you'll be able to take full advantage of the existing products & services in the blockchain ecosystem as everything is some combination of a *withdraw* (*send)* transaction & a *deposit* (*receive)* transaction.

Withdrawals (Sending) To make a payment, switch exchanges, fund a wallet, or otherwise move funds, you must initiate a "withdraw" transaction. Keep in mind that some platforms will refer to this as a "send" transaction, which is the exact same thing.

Step One

Enter a recipient or deposit address by copying the address or scanning the associated QR code (recommended method).

Step Two

Verify the recipient/deposit address is accurate. Blockchain transactions are irreversible, so if there's an error, the funds are unretrievable.

Step Three

Confirm/approve the withdrawal request. You'll likely need to enter a validation code from a 2-Factor Authentication app or confirm via email before the transaction process will initiate. If you haven't already set up additional verification, do so.

Deposits (Receiving) As in the traditional financial world, all deposits must be funded by a withdrawal from another account. In the case of digital assets, deposits are funded via withdrawal from another address or account. Just like withdrawals, some platforms will refer to deposits as a "receive" transaction. Different name, same function.

Step One

Select the "receive" function within the destination account/address, revealing your deposit address.

Step Two

Insert deposit address into the "receive" section of the address/account funding the deposit. Alternatively, provide your deposit address to the entity sending funds to your address.

Step Three

Verify the deposit/recipient address is accurate. Blockchain transactions are irreversible, so if there's an error, the funds are unretrievable.

Step Four

Unlike withdrawal transactions, you don't need to approve anything as the recipient of deposited funds. Nevertheless, it's still good form to confirm the deposit has been initiated by inspecting the transaction ID using a block explorer tool such as Blockchair or EtherScan.

Fees

All transactions incur what is known as a "transaction fee", typically paid in the native coin of its respective blockchain. For transactions made on the Bitcoin blockchain, fees are paid in BTC. For transactions made on the Ethereum network, whether it is Ethereum, or some other token, fees must be paid in ETH. Though the fee structure + fee amount varies, this general heuristic holds true for any transaction made on a native blockchain network.

Speed

It should also be kept in mind that the speed of transactions, how long it takes for them to achieve settlement finality on-chain, is often dependent on the fees paid. If you want faster transaction settlement you can opt to increase your gas fee thus "outbidding" other transactions so that yours gets greater priority & settles faster. Depending on the network, traffic, & fees paid, this process can take a few seconds or a few hours.

Not all networks suffer from slow transaction times. Certain protocols are designed + optimized for higher throughput TPS (transactions per second), resulting in faster transaction confirmations. For instance, something like Ripple Labs' XRP coin or Polygon Network's MATIC token are both designed to settle quickly & have fees that are orders of magnitude cheaper than Ethereum's. However, something like Ethereum is more optimized for decentralization + security, trading speed as a result. The quest for lower fees is one of the driving factors of the adoption of other Layer 1 smart contract protocols such as Solana, Cardano, Avalanche, & Polkadot.

Transaction Best Practices

Though relatively simple & straightforward, there are a handful of transaction best practices you should keep in mind. It can be easy to make a mistake if one isn't being mindful as they navigate the digital asset space. Observe the following suggestions to ensure your transactions flow smoothly.

QR Codes & Copy/Paste Whenever possible, you want to scan the QR code representing the deposit/receiving address. If you can't use the QR code, copy + paste it. **DO NOT** type out the address by hand. Extraordinarily bad idea. Of course, you *could* do so successfully, but why introduce an increased risk of error if you don't have to?

Network Compatibility Confirm that all funds are being sent to a compatible blockchain network. For instance, if you're going to send Bitcoin, the receiving address must be a Bitcoin compatible address. If you're sending ETH or any other ERC-20 token on the Ethereum network, it must be sent to an Ethereum based address. If the addresses involved in the transaction are not compatible, the deposited assets will be lost with no way to recover them.

Block Confirmations Different blockchains have different inherent speeds based on their design, making some blockchains faster than others due in part to the time between new blocks on the network. It is recommended that you always check the number of required confirmations specific to the address or account you're using, since some applications differ in their degree of "finality" before dubbing a transaction as confirmed. Nexo for instance requires 50 confirmations for any Ethereum based transaction. It requires six confirmations for any Bitcoin specific transaction. Once you're familiar with how many confirmations are required for the application in use you can always check a block explorer to make sure everything is moving along as it should, quelling any potential concerns of undue delays or otherwise lengthy transaction times.

Centralized Exchanges (CEXs)

At some point, much like you might use a broker to access stocks, options, or various derivatives, you'll almost certainly need to interact with an exchange to buy, sell, or trade any of these digital assets. Perhaps the quickest, easiest way to buy any digital asset, specifically Bitcoin, is via CashApp. What makes CashApp such a solid choice?

CashApp: *BTC In 1, 2, 3!*

CashApp: The Benefits

Convenience It's quick & simple to get up & running. If you're reading this, you likely have a CashApp account or you're in a position where you could create one in a few minutes. Once you've made the account, it's very simple to start buying and selling Bitcoin within the app. Just look for the Bitcoin logo, click it, and specify how much you want to purchase. Once done, you're now able to withdraw the BTC to another address or sell it for cash.

Private Custody Any Bitcoin purchased through CashApp is immediately yours since you're buying true Bitcoin - *not* a derivative instrument. This means you *own* the private keys. From the moment you buy your Bitcoin you can send it off to a different exchange or a different wallet. Nobody's going to stop you. It's actually impossible to stop you due to the asymmetric encryption engineered into the Bitcoin protocol & most other digital asset protocols for that matter.

Dollar Cost Averaging With CashApp you can set a recurring purchase to easily dollar cost average (DCA) into a long-term Bitcoin position. Whether you schedule a daily, weekly, or monthly order, just choose an amount (ex. $20/week) & your tailored order will execute automatically at predetermined intervals. You're free to change & adjust the frequency & amount as you see fit.

CashApp: The Drawbacks

Bitcoin Only As it stands right now, CashApp only allows users to buy & sell Bitcoin. If you are interested in gaining exposure to other digital assets like ETH (Ethereum), DOT (Polkadot), MANA (Decentraland) or any other coin/ token, you'll have to find them elsewhere since CashApp, at the time of this writing, is a BTC maximalist platform. Though its selection is still quite limited, Venmo, which is owned by PayPal, is another mobile payments app with built-in digital asset support.

Limited Order Types Emphasizing that it is *not* a professional-level exchange, CashApp only allows market orders (buy & sell) & limit orders (buy only). Though the added feature allowing custom buy orders is appreciated & underscores the long-term "HODL" mentality, no doubt a strategic decision by Square's Jack Dorsey, more sophisticated traders may find the lack of order types restrictive. There's no way to set custom sell orders, stop orders, or trailing stop orders.

CashApp: *Alternative Choices*

If you don't want to use CashApp, there are comparable apps delivering similar pros & cons in tow.

<u>CashApp Alternatives</u>

- Revolut
- Changelly
- Bamboo
- Venmo
- Robinhood
- Amber

Important Keep in mind that some of these platforms may not allow you private key access, meaning you're just buying a derivative of the underlying asset, NOT the true digital asset itself. Private key access is the single most important standard when considering which digital asset gateway to use. Be sure to do your diligence prior to buying through *any* platform, regardless of their reputability.

Coinbase: *The "Apple" Of Exchanges*

Coinbase: The Benefits

As far as robust *centralized* exchanges, Coinbase is likely the most well-known option available. Let's assess some of the platform's strengths.

Digital Asset Variety At the time of writing, Coinbase has more than 95 digital assets available to trade on its platform with more being added all the time. Some have criticized the rate at which Coinbase has begun to add new assets, claiming it's more of a "cash-grab" than anything else. I certainly understand that sentiment, but just be sure to do your own research (D.Y.O.R.) prior to investing as not all digital assets are created equal.

Free Money A particularly unique benefit of Coinbase is their "Earn" product which allows you to earn free crypto as a reward for spending a few minutes learning about select assets & successfully answering a few quiz questions. This elegant solution serves as an incentive for users to get familiar with the platform's new listings while also helping newcomers get some "skin in the game" in exchange for a little time & attention. I highly encourage you to get your free assets if you haven't already. Who knows how long Coinbase will continue the program post-IPO?

Advanced Order Types As any good exchange should, Coinbase features limit orders in addition to its standard market orders. If you want even more options & features like order books, depth charts & integrated TradingView charts, check out Coinbase Pro, the company's trader-centric product.

Funding Methods Be it a debit card, credit card, ACH, wire transfer, PayPal or Apple Pay, Coinbase makes funding an account convenient for all sorts of investors. Do be sure to check your country though, as funding methods differ based on region.

Coinbase: The Drawbacks

High Spreads It's well known within the crypto space that users often pay a higher price on Coinbase compared to other exchanges. This phenomenon is referred to as the "Coinbase

Premium". Granted, this premium is only a problem if you're *buying* your assets on Coinbase. You can often avoid this premium (as well as the fees) by simply trading on Coinbase *Pro*, the dedicated exchange designed for professional traders. Nevertheless, if you buy somewhere *other than* Coinbase, you can use the spread to your advantage, creating an arbitrage opportunity to sell your assets on Coinbase for the higher price, effectively capturing the premium. It's a simple yet tried & true trade - just be diligent to make sure that any fees or slippage don't render the arbitrage opportunity moot.

Poor Customer Support Historically Coinbase has had lackluster customer support. If you have an issue, be it pressing or otherwise, expect to wait several days or perhaps even weeks, before hearing anything back. In some instances, users have even had their accounts frozen or closed without any prior notice or explanation. In effort to win back the faith of its users, the firm recently announced additional live voice support specifically aimed at assisting users who're believed to have had their accounts hijacked or otherwise breached. Only time will tell how well the initiative holds up, but it's a good gesture all the same.

Coinbase: Alternative Choices

It's good practice to use a few different exchanges. Not only does it spread your risk across various platforms which, undoubtedly, have differing levels of security & resilience, but this practice may grant you access to lesser-known assets, better fees, lower spreads, greater liquidity, API integration, & more. Listed below are several exchanges that compete with Coinbase.

The Best Alternative Centralized Exchanges

- KuCoin
- Gemini
- OkEx
- Kraken
- Binance
- FTX

Decentralized Exchanges (DEXs)

The purpose of a decentralized exchange (DEX) is to allow users to trade digital assets in a *trustless* manner, meaning peer-to-peer & without any *trusted* intermediaries. DEXs provide many advantages vs their centralized counterparts, but the primary ones are privacy & the elimination of counterparty risk. Before diving into the benefits of Uniswap, arguably the most popular DEX, let's examine the Robinhood debacle of 2021.

Robinhood: A Cautionary Tale of Centralization

Centralized exchanges wield a great deal of power over user accounts & funds since they control virtually every aspect of the system. You may recall when Robinhood, a popular retail trading app, halted trading during the GME rally of the first quarter of 2021. Not only did they halt trading, but they even forcibly closed (i.e. *sold*) many of their users' open positions without any consent or prior warning. Could you imagine buying Bitcoin for ~$5,000 & suddenly the price begins to climb by hundreds of percentage points in a single week - then out of nowhere, Coinbase forcibly *sells* your Bitcoin even as prices continue to surge? I won't speak for you - but I'd have quite the urge to pull up on Mr. Armstrong & air out a few grievances!

Of course, Robinhood's PR team justified the aggressive overreach by claiming it was protecting its users. I don't buy it. Neither should you. The reality is Robinhood (& their friends over at Citadel & Melvin Capital) didn't have sufficient liquidity on hand to settle the enormous balances many users *would* have made in profits if they would have been able to continue riding the upward price action. This manipulation had the tandem effect of stifling what many Redditors affectionately refer to as the "Mother of All Short Squeezes" (MOASS) from launching a violent move upward that may have made many retail investors multi-millionaires while simultaneously triggering a cascading margin call that could have bankrupted many prominent hedge funds & trading desks integral to the modern financial system. All facts, figures, & opinions aside - should Robinhood or any other broker, centralized or otherwise, even be *capable* of such intervention?

Uniswap: DeFi's First Unicorn

Uniswap: The Benefits

More Privacy Anti-Money Laundering (AML) & Know Your Customer (KYC) regulations are the reason all centralized exchanges, brokers, banks, & financial entities require users to submit copious amounts of personally identifiable data before they're allowed to open an account. While the logic is clear &

sound on the surface, not everyone *wants* to provide so much sensitive information just to access basic services. Further, what happens if that data gets in the wrong hands? (*Hint*: Dark Web shenanigans)

The beautiful thing about DEXs - they completely solve this issue. How? Direct Web3.0 wallet integration into the DEX's underlying smart contract protocol allows you to self-custody funds throughout the entire trading process as sell/buy orders settle directly inside of your wallet.

Consequently, there's no need to provide any KYC documentation or any other personally identifiable data. Anybody can trade in a private, pseudonymous nature, assuming the user's ISP doesn't block access to the site & the DEX allows users from their region. There are some easy fixes to work around "restriction" issues though. (*Hint*: it rhymes with VPN) Do note that using a DEX allows you to maintain *pseudonymity*, **not** *anonymity*, since all transactions are still associated with the wallet addresses involved - a truism spanning *all* of crypto.

Less Trust Tired of assuming counterparty risk? DEXs fix this too. Because funds are always in your custody & there's no trusted third party or central controlling entity to intervene in the trading process, buy, sell or freeze funds, counterparty risk is effectively eliminated. Robinhood-style "protections" aren't possible on a DEX due to its fundamental design. You don't need to *trust* Coinbase or their servers to be up & active during heightened market volatility. With a true DEX, everything is done in distributed, trustless fashion at the protocol level, so odds are, barring a wild solar flare or random EMP, it will be up no matter what. In that unlikely event, there are *far* greater things to be concerned about.

Speed DEXs tend to be very quick + straightforward to operate. Though most offer advanced functionality, all "power user" features are tucked away behind alternate panels within the app. When you open most DEXs the first thing you'll see is a widget with two blanks fields: one to select the asset being "sold" & another to select the asset being "bought". Simply specify your order and hit "swap" – deed done! This minimalistic approach effectively abstracts layers of back end smart contract execution + order routing to create an intuitive UX for users, the epitome of sophistication in simplicity.

Uniswap: The Drawbacks

Fees If you're using an Ethereum-based DEX, gas fees are going to be higher than would otherwise be the case on a centralized exchange. This can be mitigated by avoiding high traffic times of day or by switching over to a higher TPS network like Matic (Polygon) or Arbitrum. If you're comfortable using bridges, check out the Polygon's Quickswap or the Solana based DEX Raydium. Fees are negligible & when combined with something like the Phantom wallet, it's a breeze.

Networks + Bridges Uniswap may be one of the most popular DEXs available, but it only works well with ERC-20 tokens. As more smart contract protocols like Solana + Polkadot gain traction, the need for other DEXs becomes apparent. Some alternatives like SushiSwap allow you to switch between networks with a click of a button, while others like Raydium require you to "bridge" your assets over before you can bounce between token standards. Polygon's website hosts a simple to use bridge to move assets between the Polygon (Matic) & Ethereum network. It's not complicated, but first-time users may find the process daunting.

Even with their unique advantages, DEXs still pose their own risks & challenges. Since there is no way to exert centralized control of the platform there is no official support if you were to have any issues. Additionally, not all DEXs are built on sound code. Some decentralized trading platforms have been exploited or hacked out of millions of customer funds. Poly Network, a cross-chain DeFi platform, was exploited to the tune of more than $600M. Romantic as "In Code We Trust!" may sound, code is still (primarily) written & audited by people. People, in most instances, happen to be human. Keep this in mind.

Dollar Cost Averaging (DCA)

The idea of small, regular investments made over extended periods of time is a very powerful concept, not just in blockchain and digital assets, but in the broader investment context.

Better Cost Basis The benefits of dollar cost averaging are several-fold. To start with, you're likely to get a much better average price. Say that over the course of a year you allocated $1,000 to invest into Ethereum. If you went all in one day when Ethereum happened to be $1,000, congrats! You've now got yourself one whole Ethereum. Well, let's say a week or two passes & the markets retrace into a decent correction. Now, instead of being valued at $1,000 that same Ethereum is only worth $500. I'm sure you would prefer to have invested that $1,000 on the day that it was $500 for one ETH instead of $1,000. Let's take it one step further. A month later one ETH is trading at $2,000. You probably feel pretty good now about your $1,000 entry. The beauty is that you can remove all price fluctuations from the equation with a properly executed DCA strategy.

If you split your $1,000 into three separate, equal payments or investments, allocating a third at $500 per ETH, you put a third in at $1,000, & a third in at $2,000, you're going to capture the average of those three distinct price levels. Over an extended period, most people significantly improve their cost basis (average entry price into any asset) if they regularly invest a consistent amount -regardless of what the price is.

Automatic Investing Setting your investments to execute automatically positions you for better long-term consistency, and thus, better long-term success. Market volatility can make it difficult to remain focused + committed to an investment plan, regardless of how sound the thesis may be. The root of this is emotional + psychological. It's easy to be excited about investing in an asset while the market climbs higher & higher. Watching your wealth multiply is quite a feeling! The moment there's a substantial decline in the value of an asset, the euphoria begins to subside as fear + worry creep in, making it much more difficult to continue observing the original plan. With your investments triggered by automatic payments, it becomes far easier to ride out the markets' more challenging moments.

Fixed Budgeting Fear of missing out is often the culprit which compels people to go all in on an investment at one time, often investing more than they can even afford. The simple act of dollar cost averaging puts one in much better position to consistently add to their portfolio without blowing their allotted budget simply because they got a little too excited about the money-making opportunity.

BECOMING THE BANK

"

If we command our wealth, we shall be rich & free.

If our wealth commands us, we shall be poor indeed…

"

Edmond Burke

You're The Bank Now

Amidst the violently rapid news cycle + whirlwind of life-enhancing gains, it's easy to overlook the fact that debit cards, credit cards, and interest-bearing savings accounts natively designed for the digital asset space are already widely available. Creating passive income streams by activating your capital via lending or staking protocols, providing liquidity as a market maker, accessing instantly approved credit lines or simply sending payments directly to someone's private wallet can all be done in seconds. But why even bother?

Benign on the surface, central banking institutions are criminal enterprises through & through. Whether laundering money for drug cartels under the guise of remittances or incentivizing local branch managers to open unauthorized shell accounts to achieve performance bonuses, both of which proving to be preferred schemes of Wells Fargo, the day's flavor of finesse is anybody's guess. The sheer brilliance of their charade is a sight to behold. As one of the world's most morally bankrupt institutions, central banks have crafted an image of trustworthiness sufficient to convince the civilization to deposit their life's earnings for little to no benefit. This rouse is built upon a "Triple-A" illusion: access, autonomy, authenticity. Want to withdraw all your funds on a holiday? Too bad. Care to conduct business with a merchant in a foreign country? Hope your payment doesn't get blocked. Ready to redeem your cash for its underlying value? There is none. It's called a dollar "bill" because it's a representation of debt on the books - not gold, not grain, but financial burden packaged as an I.O.U.

Spending Digital Assets In the Physical World: *Internet Money I.R.L*

Gone are the days of holding on to crypto simply for the sake of speculation or Dark Web use. Now more than ever people are looking for ways to use their digital assets in the real world. When it comes to spending your crypto online or at brick-and-mortar business, there are many viable solutions, most of which being debit cards or rewards credit cards. Of the several I've come across, the BitPay debit card is my first recommendation as it perfectly suits most user's needs. If you want to earn cashback, check out the BlockFi card.

BitPay: *A Blockchain Debit Card*

Existing on the MasterCard network means the BitPay card is widely accepted at most merchants without any annual or monthly service fees. There's plenty out of the box support for many of the largest crypto assets like Bitcoin, Ethereum, DAI, & even Dogecoin, while the integrated 1Inch-powered DEX means users can swap assets directly within the application, boosting functionality & greatly expanding asset compatibility. Whereas some other cards are conservative in terms of ATM withdrawal limits, BitPay leads the crowd with its generous daily allowance. If you happen to be a business owner looking to accept digital asset payments within your business, BitPay can facilitate that for you as well, an added convenience.

BitPay's main shortcoming has less to do with the product itself & more to do with Ethereum's network congestion. Since loading the card involves making a deposit, users must pay miner fees. Sometimes the fees are only a few dollars, sometimes they're $100+. I'd advise loading your card no more than once or twice a month & doing so during periods of low network traffic to avoid the fees becoming prohibitively expenses. Otherwise, the card works great for most situations, though the lack of a dedicated accounting + routing number prevents it from working in certain circumstances.

Step One

Download the BitPay app to get started.

Order your physical card within the app (Optional)

Step Two

Upon loading you'll be prompted to create a new wallet secured by a randomly generated mnemonic recovery phrase. Be sure to back this phrase up somewhere safe.

Step Three

Deposit funds to your account. The BitPay wallet supports several different assets, so be sure you're depositing to the correct account within your wallet.

Be sure to add some ETH too - you'll need it cover the network fee associated with loading your debit card prior to being able to transact.

Step Four

Once your funds have landed in your wallet, simply choose how much you want to load onto your card, making sure to have enough ETH to cover the miner fee.

Nexo: *A Blockchain Credit Card*

For those of you grimacing at the mere thought of using a *debit* card, fret not. If you seek cash back rewards & improved cash flow, I suggest checking out Nexo's credit card. It does nearly everything a traditional credit card does, but with one major distinction: dynamically adjusted credit lines. Instead of being issued a static limit based on credit score, payment history, revolving balance, etc., Nexo determines credit lines using an over-collateralization model. It is the very antithesis of how most credit accounts work & the sole reason Nexo & other blockchain based lenders can grant instantly approved credit lines with zero knowledge of or impact on credit history.

Though less common amongst most retail clients, the over-collateralization process is rather straightforward. In order to access a credit line you'll need to deposit funds to your account to serve the dual purpose of acting as collateral & to display trust worthiness in lieu of a credit score. The logic is simple. If you decide not to repay your loan, Nexo will recoup their money from your collateral deposit. Various digital assets are acceptable as collateral, each bearing different loan-to-value (LTV) ratios that influence how much credit you can access vs your deposit. Stablecoin assets like DAI + USDC have higher LTV ratios vs volatile assets like BTC + ETH. The higher the LTV, the higher the credit limit relative to collateral.

So, let's say you deposit $1,000 worth of ETH as collateral today at a LTV ratio of 50%. Instantly, you have an available credit line of $500. If Ethereum doubles in price tomorrow, so does your credit line, which is now $1,000. This dynamic credit ratio adjusts automatically & is immediately reflected on your card. However, should the value of ETH drop by 50%, so will your credit line. If your account balance drops too low relative to the requisite LTV ratio Nexo will begin to repay your loan by liquidating your collateral. This is easy to avoid by maintaining a healthy utilization ratio, monitoring drastic market swings via price alerts, & always keeping some collateral dominated in a stable asset to anchor your account's balance.

While you can readily create an account & use Nexo's services on their website & through their app, a limited rollout process means obtaining a physical card may prove difficult depending on when you're reading this. Nexo also provides cash back on nearly every purchase, but rates are lower than many competitors like the BlockFi Rewards Visa & the Gemini credit card.

Passive Income: *The Alchemy of Yield*

The astronomically high interest earnings powered by blockchain tech makes passive income opportunities one of crypto's greatest use cases – bar none. To this day I remain aghast at how few people are capitalizing on the risk-free gains ripe for the making. If ever you've considered the looming specter of inflation, fret not. This is yet another tool to help you triumph in a world of baseless fiat. Enter: the alchemy of yield.

Step One

Convert fiat into crypto using your preferred exchange or a direct gateway like Onramper.

If you wish to avoid volatility, be sure to convert into a stablecoin such as USDC or DAI.

Step Two

Deploy digital assets to a yield bearing protocol for an agreeable amount of time. With hundreds of viable options, research the following before committing to a platform:

Yield Protocols + Platforms

(Centralized Vs Decentralized)

- Nexo
- BlockFi
- Crypto.com
- Celsius

- Aave
- Compound
- Anchor
- Yearn.Fiance

Step Three

After capital has had time to earn interest there are two main choices.

Option 1: Allow yields to continue compounding & growing exponentially on autopilot.

Option 2: Withdraw funds to reinvest elsewhere.

Step Four

Reap. Rinse. Repeat.

In effort to better illustrate the power of yield alchemy, imagine the following hypothetical situation. As long-time fan of blockchain + crypto recognizing a bull market is imminent, you decide it's finally time to get some skin in the game, beginning your due diligence on a few projects that've been on your radar.

You've read the white papers, investigated the ecosystem, analyzed competitors, market fit, etc. Confident in your picks, you settle on 10 projects for which you have absolute conviction, investing $1,000 into each of their associated tokens, brining your crypto portfolio to a value of $10,000.

To your amazement, 2 years of bullish momentum have multiplied your portfolio to a total value of $100K, 10X'ing your initial investment. What an achievement & testament to your ability to assess strong fundamental value! Refusing to be complacent during a bear market, you deploy your $100,000 to an interest-bearing protocol yielding 10% annual interest compounding daily, a move that only takes a handful of minutes to execute from your phone or laptop. Just like that, you've guaranteed yourself an extra $10,000 paid to you in daily installments over the next year, *passively*. Each dollar earned automatically begins accruing additional interest in a potent feedback loop of automatic wealth creation. With such a system in place you'll have a balance of $271,790 after 10 years & $738,703 after 20 years, all from an initial investment of $10K. Behold, the alchemy of yield.

O.P.M: *The Power Of Leverage*

Other people's money. It's one of the most potent wealth generation tools ever known. Few are the fortunes that've been made without it. Why? It takes money to make money. Obviously. Here's the thing: it doesn't have to be *your* money.

Debt is an economic tool, and like any tool, it should be respected & applied appropriately. Whether it be a direct loan like a credit line or an abstraction in the form of margin, debt allows for maximum gain with minimum capital. With this financial leverage one may increase their purchasing power, boost on-hand liquidity, & access more profitable opportunities.

Like everything else we've discussed, borrowing + lending products come in many flavors, but I prefer Nexo as the best all-around platform. Generous double digit APY for major assets & stablecoins, instant loans & collateral swaps are easily accessible via Nexo's website & sleek mobile application. Add in $375M insurance & dozens of financial licenses across dozens of states + territories & it's a no brainer. While other platforms like Celsius support a wider range of assets, too much variety can be a hinderance to platform stability as more volatility variables are introduced. In most cases this isn't a problem, but it can play a factor during hectic market movements. If for some reason you don't want to use Nexo but want a similar offering, look at Crypto.com, Celsius, + BlockFi.

Portfolio Management: *Truth In Numbers*

Detailed portfolio management is a critical component of assessing overall profit/loss performance. While a basic spreadsheet could certainly suffice, consider using the FTX app, formerly known as Blockfolio. You can reference their website to get an idea, but it's only available as a mobile application at the time of writing. You can use the app to buy + trade crypto, but I suggest using it strictly as a focused tool for documenting all your buy + sell orders, as well as any transfers. If you're comfortable with it & happen to use Kraken, Coinbase, Gemini, or any other supported exchange you can even connect your portfolio directly via API to track your transactions automatically. Take care to be as precise as possible should you take the time to log things manually. Be sure to include the date, time, order types, fees, price & size of your trades.

BITCOIN:
THE ORIGINAL
CRYPTO

"

The real problem with conventional currency is all the trust that's required to make it work. The history of fiat currencies is full of breaches of that trust.

"

Satoshi Nakamoto

How Bitcoin Works

Bitcoin is powered and created through a process known as "Mining". Miners contribute computational resources to the network in effort to confirm pending transactions by adding them to the Bitcoin ledger. Using Proof of Work (PoW) consensus, every 10 minutes miners must "work" to solve a complex SHA-256 hash equation that confirms the contents of the block to be valid before new BTC is minted + given to the miner in the form of a block reward.

Distributed: *Power To The People*

Even as concentrated pools dominate the industry, mining can be done by anyone - assuming you have the right hardware. In the early days mining could be done on a consumer grade computer. Now, dedicated machines known as ASICs (application specific integrated circuits) + access to relatively cheap energy are requisite to be a profitable miner. Still, anyone dedicated enough can join in.

Proof Of Work: *Will Work For BTC*

Since inception Bitcoin has used a proof of work consensus mechanism. Though critics have cited Bitcoin as an environmental threat due to massive energy requirements, the large power draw gives the network it's tremendous security, its proponents tending to appreciate the physical commitment requisite to secure the network. Some have even described Bitcoin + PoW as "...the ability to convert energy - both technological + physical - into a scarce monetary good that cannot be censored, confiscated or copied…" How poetic.

Block Rewards: *Ingenious Incentives*

Issued every ~10 minutes, the block reward mints a fixed number of BTC that eventually enter circulation when miners sell the "virgin" coins. The reward is programmatically reduced by 50% every 4 years until 21M BTC have been minted. This supply schedule drives price action + encourages miners to add hash power, boosting network security in a virtuous cycle.

In theory, mining can be done by anybody, but the reality is quite different. Given the moat-like economies of scale that now surround the industry, it is far more difficult for any solo entity to profitably mine BTC. It *can* be done, but it's almost certainly going to be a money-losing endeavor unless millions are invested into the operation. For most who remain adamant on mining, it would be advised to begin by joining a larger pool to keep startup costs to a minimum.

Nodes: *Smooth Operator*

What's more feasible than mining is for somebody to run a node. Instead of mining + minting new BTC, ardent Bitcoin believers can run their own node, a continuously updating record of all transactions on the Bitcoin blockchain - independently owned + operated by whoever so desires to spin one up. Nodes aren't responsible for solving any of the SHA-256 equations required to mint new BTC, but rather, they host + transmit an additional copy of the greater Bitcoin blockchain ledger. This allows node operators to have direct access to the global Bitcoin ledger. Yet another expression of commitment to the "Don't trust, verify" nature of crypto. Imagine if you could whip up a node that gave you access to the entire transaction history of JP Morgan or BlackRock. Pretty powerful, indeed.

The proof of work consensus mechanism makes it difficult to attack or unilaterally control the mining network. Due to high energy demands, attackers would have to allocate a substantial amount of resources + energy to have a shot at launching a successful 51% attack on the Bitcoin network. Similarly attack resistant, though for different reasons, proof of stake consensus requires a sizeable amount of capital to attack the network.

The key distinction to note is that it's easier for somebody to begin mining in a PoS system as they could allocate the needed funds as a direct investment into the ecosystem, pool their funds together with other motivated investors, or they could join a larger pool established by a CEX or other large entity to contribute a fraction of the network's requirement for solo staking.

Block Rewards: *A Grand Prize*

Bitcoin's block reward mechanism is directly associated with the famed four year "halving" cycle, which historically, has driven the entire crypto market in terms of bullish appreciation phases & bearish markdown phases. Every four years (approximately), the block reward issuance rate gets cut in half. This four-year halving schedule reduces the velocity of new Bitcoin issuance until it reaches the 21 million BTC target.

When Bitcoin debuted 50 BTC were minted every 10 minutes as a subsidy to reward miners for securing the network, a subsidy known as the block reward. In 2012 the block reward was reduced by 50%, with only 25 new BTC minted every 10 minutes. 2016 saw the reward drop to 12.5 BTC & 2020 halved the issuance down to 6.25 BTC. In 2024, the block reward will decrease by another 50% with the halving cycle continuing until all 21 million BTC are minted.

The cyclical issuance reduction puts significant pressure on Bitcoin's supply, the resulting supply shock often having a notable impact on the price of BTC due to the ensuing demand shock as new waves of adopters learn about the asset's programmatic scarcity for the first time. Or perhaps as they *appreciate* the asset's programmatic scarcity for the first time.

Newly minted "virgin" Bitcoin comes onto the free market as miners sell their awarded allotment to cover operating expenses. Of course, some of these miners are holding on to their BTC as a long-term investment, but there remains a certain amount of turnover necessary for these miners to remain operationally solvent, let alone profitable.

Any BTC used, custodied, or otherwise interacted with after miners sell them to the open market can no longer be deemed "virgin" coins. Some exchanges & custodians have even gone as far as to ban or reject "tainted" BTC, coins that have been involved in illicit transactions according to interpretations of on-chain data. I add this simply to acknowledge that the argument of BTC being perfectly fungible isn't entirely correct based on the policies of certain entities within the digital asset space. While most users will never be burdened by tainted coins, there are several ways to "clean" them should you need to. (*Hint*: It rhymes with "mixer")

Bitcoin's Tech: *An Overview*

The Merits Of Bitcoin's Technology

Stable + Time Tested Being the original crypto currency, Bitcoin has weathered the test of time more than any other digital asset in existence, managing an uptime of more than 99.98%. Since launch the network has spent less than 16 hours offline, the last outage happening in March 2013. For nearly a decade now the Bitcoin protocol hasn't missed a beat, even as ever-increasing sums of value flow in, hash rates grow & transaction volumes rise. Bitcoin's impeccable uptime is a marvel of distributed networking engineering.

Secure + Attack Resistant With intentions to replace the fiat system & emerge as a long-term store of value, Bitcoin was designed with security top of mind. Rivaling its stability, the network has a marvelous history of remaining free from hacks or loss of user funds. From its immutable, distributed, time-dependent triple entry ledger mechanism, to its 51% attack resistance & sybil resistance, Bitcoin's groundbreaking innovations have kept the network secure while inspiring an entire industry of distributed cryptographic protocols in its wake.

Deeply Decentralized Though it may be surprising to some, not all blockchains optimize for decentralization. Bitcoin allows for anybody to run a full node to broadcast a copy of the blockchain, removing any need to trust that things are operating as they should. The easier it is to run a node, the more users *will* run a node, which further distributes the network, ultimately boosting overall resilience + trustlessness in the process.

Researched + Studied Bitcoin captured the consciousness of the cypherpunk community when Satoshi Nakamoto announced the project on the legendary message board. All these years later, Bitcoin still has a fervent community of supporters who've dedicated their entire lives to enriching the protocol. Whether it be scholars like Saiffedean Ammous, philosophers like Robert Breedlove, or venture capitalists like Anthony Pompliano, Bitcoin has an abundance of data, graphs, facts, figures, anecdotes, & essays thoroughly assessing the merits & risks of the protocol.

The Downfalls Of Bitcoin's Technology

Low Throughput Bitcoin's transaction throughput is appallingly low relative to other blockchains like Litecoin, Dash, or even Ethereum. Such a limitation isn't dire though. Bitcoin was designed with a particular focus on decentralization + privacy, both of which led to engineering choices that result in the network's less than stellar TPS. Enter: the Lightning Network, a Layer 2 scaling solution purpose built to increase Bitcoin's transaction capacity. Though slow, adoption of the Lightning network steadily continues to grow with time. Even Twitter announced plans to enable a BTC "tip" feature into the platform built atop the Lightning network.

Limited Functionality As it stands at the time of publishing, the Bitcoin network is rather constrained in its utility. Other than storing wealth, which may be all it ever needs do to, I happen to think we'll see more traction of multi-signature Bitcoin wallets used for ESCROW purposes. Technically, there are ways in which smart contracts can be built using Bitcoin's protocol, but it's currently far more limited than anything you'd see with a native smart contract platform like Ethereum or Solana.

Energy Intensive It's no secret that PoW consensus models require an immense amount of energy. Some major new outlets have published pieces explaining why Bitcoin is going to ruin the environment if it continues pressing ahead at its current pace. These are mostly exaggerated works of FUD intended to manipulate price by manipulating public perception. Assuming Bitcoin survives + continues using its current PoW design, it could act as a key catalyst driving renewables adoption as jurisdictions create subsidies to attract miners seeking lower power cost, thus encouraging the growth of the sector within their region. Oh, the irony.

A Walled Garden It remains difficult for other blockchains to interoperate with Bitcoin in any complex or nuanced manner. Granted, the difficulty is due in part to the secure nature of Bitcoin as its primary purpose is not extensive composability but to trustlessly + securely store value in the most decentralized manner possible. The best workaround integration at present is wrapped Bitcoin (WBTC), a tokenized version of BTC enabling compatible chains to host + use Bitcoin as if it were a native token. The way this works is straightforward. Using the wrapper of choice, be it an Ethereum compatible wrapper like WBTC or a Ren wrapper like rBTC, users deposit BTC as 1:1 collateral for the wrapped version of their choice. Some purists have cautioned against wrapping or otherwise swapping pure BTC for a tokenized version, but so far, things have worked out fine. Nevertheless, consider all the potential risks before wrapping BTC or any other digital asset.

Bitcoin's Team: *An Evaluation*

Strengths Of Bitcoin's Team

Proven Track Record Historically, any Bitcoin Improvement Proposals (BIPs) or other upgrades to the protocol have happened without major hiccups. Some could argue that bug-free updates shouldn't be applauded, but rather expected. I disagree. Science, especially technology, is often a trial + error feedback loop pushing innovation forward in a messy way. Even given the practice of refining code on beta test networks prior to mainnet launch, there's always a risk of something breaking. The diligence, patience & restraint of Bitcoin's core developer community deserves kudos for maintaining such an immaculate track record of updates + upgrades.

Weak Leadership How could weak leadership be beneficial? Considering most Bitcoin purist are deeply convicted about never putting too much trust, faith or power in any single entity, it makes sense, the core idea being the mitigation of counterparty risk. When Satoshi, whether one person (unlikely) or a pseudonymous collective of interested parties (highly likely) walked away from the project it created more than a power vacuum – it created a *trust* vacuum. Nobody in the Bitcoin ecosystem looks to any single leader for guidance or answers on what should happen next with the network. As a result of this leaderless community, far more coordination + effort is required from contributors + developers as they coordinate efforts out of innate desire rather than being driven + corralled by any central authority or dominate personality.

Weaknesses Of Bitcoin's Team

Weak Leadership For all the "crypto-credo" benefits of maintaining decentralized organization, a lack of quality leadership can prove problematic. In the case of Bitcoin, the absence of a strong, inspiring, central voice crafting a powerful vision & roadmap intended to guide the core team + broader community has left the protocol stagnant, seemingly incapable of pushing towards the next level. Many would object, claiming

Bitcoin has already achieved it final form. Though I appreciate such perspective, I respectfully disagree. The protocol has made extraordinary progress since Satoshi's exit, but a more coordinated effort would likely improve the project + accelerate mass adoption.

Small Ethereum has spawned a massive ecosystem of hundreds, if not thousands of sticky products + innovative services as developers rush to build with languages like Solidity & skillfully compose dApps leveraging the interoperable power of smart contract protocols. This boom of new user activity + product adoption is severely lacking with Bitcoin. Why? At its core Bitcoin has one function: store value by serving as the world's best example of non-violent money – a noble + needed cause that it absolutely excels at.

Natively, there's not much happening to bring greater utility to the network in the form of slick UX, high retention offerings. There are interesting ideas being worked on for sure, such as the *Sovryn* platform aiming to bring DeFi to Bitcoin, Jack Mallers' *Strike* app making BTC payments as easy as using CashApp, or Adam Curry's Podcast 2.0 standard which intends to integrate usage-based micropayments on the Lightning network to help decentralize podcasting. All of these are great ideas, they simply lack substantial traction at *this* moment. By no means does Bitcoin need some game-changing app or product to fulfil its mission, but I'm sure it wouldn't hurt.

Complacency The debate rages on. "*It's not broken. We don't need to change anything. Bitcoin was designed perfectly out the gate*!" When a technology emerges with vigor to become the standard, but subsequently fails to evolve, opportunities are created for newer technologies to come along and supplant that incumbent. It's easier for newcomers to innovate as they build atop the strengths of previous generations.

Such a precession is spurring a growing body of believers compelled by a growing body of evidence suggesting Ethereum could replace Bitcoin as a store of value (SOV). Plainly stated, Bitcoin is absolutely stagnant, technologically speaking. Should it hope to maintain hegemony of the crypto market, it must innovate. It's no longer a debate that Ethereum has a wider array of utility. Increasingly favorable tokenomics post EIP-1559 coupled with the "Triple Point Asset" thesis means the #2 cryptocurrency by market cap could soon become #1.

Tribalistic Many members of the Bitcoin community, be they core developers or ardent users, constantly project the notion that anything other than Bitcoin is a "shit coin". To be fair, most digital assets available on the market today *are* low quality & *won't* stand the test of time. Nevertheless, this "Bitcoin-or-bust" mentality is arrogant & assumes immaculate infallibility, in turn inhibiting informed improvement.

Winner Take All There's a common belief that the only wise crypto investment is BTC as all other cryptocurrencies eventually wither away into nothingness & Bitcoin eats the world whole. Sounds epic, & though very romantic, it's very shortsighted. Sure, BTC is by far the *safest* crypto investment one can make right now, but that's because of its appeal as the solution to fiat more than anything else, though its market dominance, recognizability & track record certainly contribute.

It is far wiser to approach the blockchain sector from a wholistic, interdisciplinary vantage, rather than one of competition & monopolistic outcomes. It's rare that zero-sum, winner-take all games are appropriate or valid, regardless of the context. There will be many dominant players when the digital asset ecosystem reaches maturity, not just one. The industry is an evolving amalgam of nested subsectors weaving into a larger expanse of possibilities. If someone can't see that by now, they just aren't going to make it.

The Economics Of Bitcoin:

Tokenomics

The Bullish Case For Bitcoin

Fair Distribution Bitcoin benefited from an immaculate conception as no amount of BTC was set aside for developers, early investors or any other privileged group. From day one all coins were accessible to those willing to put in work & secure the network via mining. Since the only way to sustain & grow the network was by crowdsourcing hardware, early miners were handsomely rewarded by the generous 50 BTC block reward present at launch.

Fixed Supply + Issuance Schedule The four-year block reward halving cycle is integral to Bitcoin's past, present, & future success, driving the bull and bear markets for all of crypto. As the block reward reduces by 50% every four years, so does the issuance rate of new BTC, putting deflationary pressure on the asset & causing a supply shock as the total supply approaches a the 21M ceiling. Assuming demand stays constant, the inherit scarcity catalyzes price upward as investors seek out appreciating assets in a world dominated by debased currencies.

The Bearish Case For Bitcoin

Limited Utility The fact that Bitcoin is an immaculate store of value is clear. The issue? What happens to BTC should another asset come along that is on par with BTC as a SoV but also brings greater utility in tow? Obviously, this wouldn't spell the immediate downfall of BTC, but I'd wager value would get siphoned away from the network.

Proof of Work Consensus Bitcoin's received plenty of flack for the energy consumption of PoW mining. Aside from the incentive tradeoffs & technical hurdles, why not adopt another consensus method? Principles. Bitcoin has flourished because of its strict adherence to its original code base. A pivot to a new consensus mechanism would be seen by the community as too drastic + risky at best, utter betrayal at worst.

Post 21M At present the block reward subsidy is a beautifully balanced inventive for miners to continue securing the network. What happens after 21M BTC are minted? Based on the 10-minute block times, estimates project the final Bitcoin will be mined sometime around 2140, more than 100 years from today. Such a time horizon allows for adoption + price to increase parabolically. In this scenario, it's probable that transactions fees alone will be sufficient compensation to motivate miners to continue securing the network. Alternatively, there could be substantial changes made to the consensus mechanism & fee structure of Bitcoin. Even with the game theory married with some of the industry's brightest minds speculating, there simply isn't enough data to know how things will play out.

Bitcoin's Evolving Narrative

The vision to replace fiat was clear and sound at Bitcoin's inception. The Great Recession of '08 still rippling outward, blockchain lacked significant real-world adoption when Satoshi

Nakamoto introduced Bitcoin as "Peer-To-Peer Digital Electronic Cash". Though this prospect remains a possibility, time + markets have deemed BTC more akin to gold-like hedge than anything else. The difference between now and then? A $1T+ digital asset market has emerged alongside a robust DeFi ecosystem powered largely by stablecoins built atop smart contract blockchains like Ethereum, not to mention the rapidly growing world of verifiable authenticity in the form of NFTs. Nevertheless, Bitcoin still holds the bulk of the market's value. In no uncertain terms, Bitcoin aims to fix the current monetary system.

"

The future life expectancy of an idea or technology is proportional to its current age.

The longer something has been around, chances are the longer it will survive.

"

The Lindy Effect

Bitcoin's Resilience Over Time

As the original crypto, Bitcoin faced the brunt of negativity levied toward the digital asset sector in the early days. From doubts about the tech's capabilities to fears of BTC empowering criminals - the FUD was real. Ultimately, every burgeoning asset class must traverse the "Four Phases of Mass Adoption" traversing its share of criticism along the way. Bitcoin endured + set the stage for its successors.

Concerns Of Legitimacy: *Criminals Only*

Even in 2021 some remain skittish about crypto + digital assets, erroneously claiming most users are criminals while insinuating the asset class lacks legitimate applications or traction. Bitcoin was an invaluable tool for such a cohort. Absolutely. But therein lies a powerful history lesson in disguise.

Criminals are *always* among the earliest adopters of new technologies as they search for an edge against their combatants + enemies. Powered by BTC payments, the Silk Road launched in 2011 as the Dark Web's premier marketplace for illicit contraband. Also a vector for white-collar crime, many used BTC & crypto to push elaborate Ponzi schemes like BitConnect + OneCoin. As regulatory bodies pour more attention than ever into the sector, nefarious schemes are far less prevalent & are now an exception opposed to the rule. Still,

Bitcoin shoulders the brunt of the industry's PR damage for its juvenile record.

Lack Of Regulation: *Oversight Issues*

New assets are usually slow to gain adoption due to an absence of regulatory guidance. Though some may reject outside intervention, regulations ease the minds of users + encourage new, compliant development. Unfortunately, lack of major oversight led to several exchanges collapsing and losing user funds.

The most notable failures involved losses of $500M & $190M by Mt.Gox & QuadrigaCX, respectively. The former event was seemingly due to a technical issue which resulted in customers losing their assets, whereas the latter incident was far more mysterious, involving rumors of the CEO faking his death to disappear after client accounts were drained.

Even as a supporter of decentralization + free markets, its clear that regulatory oversight has its benefits, the most significant being *clarity*. In any asset class, *especially* emerging ones, plainly stated + well defined rules entice new entrants into the field as they build, develop, and push forward free from worries that regulators will introduce sudden changes that could place them on the wrong side of the law, thus jeopardizing their efforts. First, clarity arrives, *then* the industry booms with new companies creating new products & offering new services as they leverage new business models.

Unproven Tech: *Debug*

Though new tech often brings new challenges, some bugs are more impactful than others. In 2010 an "overflow" exploit created 184B BTC, leading to a "soft-fork" five hours later. The 2017 "Bitcoin War" over block size + transaction speed fractured the community, leading to a "hard fork" birthing BCH + BSV.

The overflow exploit was one of Bitcoin's first true tests of resilience. The hack took advantage of the way large integers were handled. Apparently, inputs over a certain size triggered an overflowing output, resulting in the massive quantities of BTC produced. To fix the issue Satoshi created a soft fork of the original code that patched the overflow error & eliminated the extraneous BTC, all without forking the entire network chain.

In contrast, the block debate was a civil war within the community about how much data should be packaged inside of each individual block on the Bitcoin blockchain. On the surface, the premise was simple. Larger blocks would allow the network to process more transactions at lower cost, but it would make it more difficult for operators to run a full node. Smaller blocks would improve neutrality + decentralization, with the tradeoff of speed + transaction cost. Of course, there were other nuances to the discussion, but that's the bird's eye vantage. The result?

A hard fork forcing the community to pick sides: small block, decentralized Bitcoin or big-block, transaction-centric Bitcoin Cash?

"

Technology shapes society, and society shapes technology.

"

Robert White

Why Bitcoin Is Thriving

Bitcoin tends to experience booms + busts according to the four-year halving cycle. Nevertheless, there are countless factors contributing to the current growth of the crypto asset. Public companies and massive financial institutions have become Bitcoin bulls while crypto native firms are partnering with pro sports leagues left and right. All the while, central banks continue to print fiat in one last Hail Mary "hurrah!"

Macro Factors: *The Big Picture*

Much of Bitcoin's present success is a result of big picture developments. The most consistent driver of price is the four-year halving schedule. The other dominant macro factor helping BTC shine - quantitative easing (QE). As more fiat enters circulation increasing numbers of macro investors are opting to preserve their purchasing power via BTC.

Since March of 2020, over 20% of all US dollars in circulating supply were printed. In 2020 alone the US Federal Reserve, which is a private company, not a governmental organization, pumped an average of over $27 billion into the economy every 24 hours as part of various bailout programs + stimulus packages. Quite the per diem!

The viscous cycle of bailouts, money printing, + low or even *negative* interest rates have kept easy money flowing, hence the "up and to the right" nature of the markets for the past several decades, a blessing indeed for those poised to ride the wave. Nevertheless, such policies are bandages for a leaking aorta. Eventually, its effects will be seen, symptoms like inflation already beginning to show.

Contrary to popular believe, hyperinflation is unlikely to happen first, instead being preempted by deflation. As various fiat currencies begin to tumble around the globe at differing rates stronger denominations will rocket up in demand as they absorb the value of weakening pairs. Only after a currency pair has appreciated via deflation should hyperinflation be expected in a "last fiat standing" scenario.

Keynesian thinkers might explain why such drastic monetary + fiscal policies are needed to maintain a harmonious global economy, citing the massive fallout that would ensue if major institutions were left to fail. The irony? Ignoring + delaying the financial reset is only going to compound + supercharge the collapse.

If bankers + policymakers allow the bottom to fall out, it will be a strategic maneuver to consolidate power & influence as major entities are acquired for pennies on the dollar by *colossal* conglomerates going on the shopping spree of the century as they position themselves for the next millennia of dominance.

Institutional Adoption: *Smart Money*

In 2020 MicroStrategy ignited the corporate treasury play for BTC, Tesla + Mass Mutual following in 2021. The "smart money" continues to flow in via ETFs + ETPs, while numerous crypto products debut from firms like Goldman Sachs, Fidelity, + JPMorgan.

Day by day increasing numbers of traditional money managers + investors like Ray Dalio, Steven Druckenmiller, Paul Tudor Jones, & Scaramucci acknowledge the house of cards that is the global financial market, going on record recommending Bitcoin as one of the greatest hedges available against inflation + currency devaluation, specifically that of the US dollar. This is very different sentiment than we saw even 4 years ago, let alone at Bitcoin's inception.

Institutions, wealth firms + large companies making the crypto pivot by offering products for their accredited clients to gain exposure isn't mere self-preservation, but rather a desire to satisfy client demand + recognition that cash is one of the worst plays given the current environment.

Take Mass Mutual for example, an insurance giant whose entire business model is contingent upon risk mitigation. If an insurance firm decides to put $100 million into Bitcoin, they must deem it a prudent decision in the interest of risk mitigation, a stark contrast compared to something like Tesla converting some of its treasury. Why? It's a well-known fact that Tesla struggles to make money selling cars, instead profiting largely from selling carbon credits. A short-term bullish bet on BTC for an easy few million dollars was a no brainer for the tech company. Funny enough, even as Musk ~~triggered~~ sold the Q2 2021 dip, not a Satoshi was reported leaving the accounts of Mass Mutual.

It's not Bitcoin's technology that's changed, but rather the Lindy Effect coming into play. Bitcoin has survived for over a decade & for each new day it withstands the test of time, the greater chance it has of staying around even longer. It's a display of humility + wisdom that these individuals + institutions acknowledge the need to reassess the macro environment to better evaluate best options.

Visibility: *All PR Is Good PR*

Whether it be FTX's massive marketing push, Coinbase going public or US senators like Cynthia Lummis disclosing her crypto ownership - Bitcoin + digital assets have greater visibility and accessibility than ever before. The popularity of Bitcoin credit cards + native integrations with PayPal + Square means users don't have to HODL if they don't want to. It's clear that 2021 has been a boon for blockchain PR.

For years exchanges have been among the most notable players in sector, but they've never had direct partnerships with non-crypto entities, hence the gravity of recent endorsement +

sponsorship trends. Sam Bankman-Fried's FTX is leading the charge as 2021 has seen the firm sponsor the TSM esports team, sign ambassador deals across multiple pro sports leagues recruiting Steph Curry, Trevor Lawrence, & Tom Brady, even acquiring naming rights to the Miami Heat stadium. These PR moves are substantial especially when considering the history of crypto interest plummeting alongside price in bear markets. Now that FTX & their contemporaries are paying a premium for awareness, the general interest in digital assets is likely to be higher than ever before even, perhaps even staving off the brutal "crypto winter" as blockchain technologies & projects remain at the forefront of the collective conscious.

Why Bitcoin Will Prosper

The Lindy Effect posits that the longer something has been around, the longer it is likely to stay around. Bitcoin could have failed already, yet it hasn't. For each day Bitcoin remains standing, it's chances for long-term survival increases. Bitcoin will see greater regulation which will bring greater innovation which will bring in greater adoption. From where things stand, Bitcoin is an "All or Nothing" technology leaning closer to "All" than "Nothing". To be clear - Bitcoin will prosper.

Public Policy: *Playing By The Rules*

Regulatory oversight will undoubtedly create winners and losers as governments decide how they want to steer the crypto industry. Whether it leans more laissez faire or favors the more controlled, dominating side, we will have to see. In either case, two things are certain. First, greater guidance clears the way for greater competition + thus better choices for Bitcoin ETFs, ETPs, 401K s, etc. once policymakers provide informed Bitcoin + crypto guidelines. Second, should quantitative easing continue unabated, expect more countries to adopt BTC as legal tender. If "hyper Bitcoinization" is the future, crypto regulation comes in tow.

Financial Applications: *Bitcoin as Money*

El Salvador's move to officially recognize Bitcoin as a national currency has been divisive to say the least. No matter how the experiment goes, tremendous ramifications will be playing out over the coming years. On one hand, the decision raises the viability of mass adoption as countries seeking greater autonomy legitimize the assets' use as a unit of account + store of value. Perhaps even more attractive to these pioneering countries is the profit potential of large scale BTC accumulation.

On the other hand, the likes of the IMF + World Bank hate to see ascending nations reclaim their economic sovereignty. Finding states on the verge of total financial ruin before swooping in with a predatory loan that assures allegiance is their preferred modus operandi. Such methodology explains why the BIS rejected El Salvador's request for help in implementing the Bitcoin standard yet champions CBDCs. What a coincidence that the price of BTC collapsed by ~20% on Bitcoin's inaugural day as a national currency.

Social Drivers: *Community + Tech*

Large scale social behaviors will determine Bitcoin's fate. As the halving cycle drives price while incentivizing network security, status games coupled with a desire for acceptance will push Bitcoin operations + crypto businesses to go carbon-negative, ultimately accelerating green energy use. More interest in crypto means more investments toward educating consumers about the technology + its possibilities. Such knowledge may drive BTC adoption when compared against CBDCs.

Institutions such as Argo Blockchain, organizations like Michael Saylor + Elon Musk's Bitcoin Mining Council, & events like the "The 'B' Word" conference hosted by Jack Dorsey + Cathy Wood in July 2021 clearly communicate Bitcoin's need for an elegant solution to its energy consumption issues. Though a phenomenal hedge against fiat + endless quantitative easing, institutions will remain on the sideline until they feel confident Bitcoin fits into an energy compliance framework that satisfies their green mandates. Otherwise, firms risk political + PR blowback. The entire crypto market will need to align with the green politics of the times before major public entities join en masse.

"

We tend to overestimate the effect of a technology in the short run and underestimate the effect in the long run.

"

Roy Amara

ETHEREUM: THE SMART CONTRACT STANDARD

"

Bitcoin is great as a form of digital money, but it's scripting language is too weak for any kind of serious advanced applications to be built on top...

"

Vitalik Buterin

How Ethereum Works

Bitcoin set the stage by heralding a new era of computing, cryptography, & digitally native systems. Nevertheless, Bitcoin's core design objective, cryptographically securing the economic value of the world's first mathematically verifiable scarce asset in a natively digital format, means it's not easily programmable. Technically, you *can* build smart contracts applications on top of the Bitcoin blockchain – multi-signature key management is an example of this - but it's not nearly as effective, efficient, or expressive as is building atop the Ethereum blockchain with the Solidity language or even via the Ethereum Virtual Machine (EVM) emulator. That being said, let's take a moment to assess the merits of Ethereum's technology.

Proof of Stake: *Efficient Incentives*

Instead of using computational miners ala Proof-of-Work (PoW), Ethereum2.0 relies upon a Proof-of-Stake (PoS) mechanism stipulating validators must stake 32+ ETH in escrow-esque fashion to secure the network via block proposal & attestation. Along with reduced energy demands, PoS better incentivizes good actors, reduces hardware requirements & helps support sharding, a key component of ETH2.0's scaling solution.

Though viewed by some as a pivot, PoS is effectively a *requirement* for ETH2.0 & was conceived of early on as a necessary adjustment to allow Ethereum to scale to the throughput required for long-term viability as a smart contract platform processing thousands of transactions a second. Much of Ethereum's problems stem from the low transaction throughput of Ethereum's PoW model. When switched to PoS, ETH2.0's sharding framework enables far better throughput & scaling.

Alignment of incentives also happens to improve with the PoS approach. If ETH2.0 validators try to behave maliciously, proposing or attesting for malicious or incorrect blocks, they will get "slashed" & lose a portion of their staked ETH - a costly penalty. The more a validator stakes, the more they have at risk. In many ways, PoS is a far better way to incentivize cooperation across the network compared to PoW.

Ethereum's Tech: *An Overview*

The Merits Of Ethereum's Technology

Programmable + Turing Complete From a high level, broad strokes perspective, all "Turing Complete" means is that Ethereum's coding language has more expressivity & logic. This expressivity is what allows people to create such nuanced & specific programs, dApps & smart contracts using Ethereum.

Composable + Interoperable Smart contracts are often called "money Legos" because of how easily they allow financial applications to be built. One person could build a smart contract that functions as a savings wallet that dictates "If you deposit 'X' amount of 'Y' asset, you receive 'Z' yield. Somebody else takes that base layer component & integrates it into a wallet application. Now, that wallet has the same savings & yield functionality as the separate smart contract because they were able to integrate it into their new program just like an API. This "Lego" nature allows things to be built & iterated upon far more quickly than would otherwise be the case.

Ecosystem Development Ethereum is responsible for kicking off the smart contract & dApp segment inside the digital asset sector in much the same way that Bitcoin is responsible for putting blockchain at the top of everybody's mind. Anytime you hear about an "altcoin" or an application built on top of a distributed blockchain ledger, there's an extraordinarily high chance it's built on Ethereum. Of course, other blockchain's exist & have similar features to what Ethereum offers, but until a competing blockchain like Polkadot, Solana or Cardano can convincingly entice developers & *retain* users, Ethereum will remain the segment's clear leader.

Energy Friendly Consensus It's no secret - PoW uses a lot of energy. However, the *impact* of energy used is significantly blown out of proportion as a tool to steer the broader markets in a direction most advantageous & profitable for larger participants (i.e. "smart money"). If you were to *really* assess the energy impact of, let's say, the traditional banking system, tech companies mining for rare Earth metals, or even the energy consumed by the Netflix-dominated film industry, PoW mining is *far* less of an issue. Still, PoS is a more efficient consensus mechanism.

The Downfalls Of Ethereum's Technology

Substantial Update Roadmap Citing Bitcoin's fundamental code base as complete, critics express concerns about Ethereum's seemingly perpetual beta state. For the most part, that's a fair & valid critique. As I see it, occasionally things are so ambitious, be it in scale, scope or simply at a technical level, that the only viable way for it to come to fruition is by breaking it down into smaller pieces, releasing chunks at a time while steadily developing & tweaking things on the back end until final form is achieved.

Look at Tesla's "autopilot" feature. No doubt, it has been integral to the company's early EV market advantage & a key selling point for would-be Model "X" owners despite its *live* software being in ongoing beta development for years. Granted, flaws in Tesla's software have resulted in the loss of human life on more than a handful of occasions, while the worst thing to happen to Ethereum was a hack that was ultimately undone via controversial chain-state rollback (we'll discuss in more detail later). I digress...

As of press time, Ethereum is *technically* in beta. Though the stakes *aren't* life & death with Ethereum, it is still *livelihood & security* for those choosing to entrust their capital with the protocol & any products, services, or tokens running on top of it. Things have gone relatively smoothly for many years, most recently with the implementation of EIP-1559 during the London upgrade. Still, every time there's a major update there's also an opportunity for a major flaw, exploit or hiccup that *could* spell disaster for the protocol & the wider ecosystem intertwined with it.

Smart Contract Vulnerability Since anybody can create a smart contract, often regardless of their programming prowess, many low-quality contracts & dApps make it to market. The reality is that many of these lower tier offerings have never endured a proper code audit prior to going live & as such, can be particularly vulnerable to exploitation by savvy developers & hackers.

Low Quality, Low Security Projects The expansive ecosystem spawned into existence by Ethereum bears with it a two-sided blade. Frankly, a lot of projects just aren't good, having poor code bases & poor security. A common phenomenon that strikes me as quite telling is the propensity for developers within the Ethereum community to build & contribute code anonymously, a trend I rarely see inside of the Bitcoin development scene. Of course, anonymity is a basic right & is sometimes done for good reason. Be it self-preservation, altruism, or a pure aversion to notoriety or scrutiny, I can understand why someone may not want to be publicly involved with a project. Regardless, it must be acknowledged that anonymity brings a bevy of malicious actors building projects up only to “rug pool" or otherwise “exit scam”, hurting many unassuming users in the process.

Ethereum’s Team: *An Evaluation*

Strengths Of Ethereum’s Team

Strong Organization & Leadership Imagine if Satoshi Nakamoto was around to guide Bitcoin daily, actively shaping the protocol’s future. Well, Ethereum has that in Vitalik Buterin, the project’s polyglot brainiac co-founder. Though no longer directly involved with the protocol, note that Polkadot’s Dr. Gavin Wood & Cardano’s Dr. Charles Hoskinson co-founded Ethereum alongside Vitalik, the former inventing the Solidity contract language & penning the project’s “Yellow Paper”, the later pivoting to build atop the Haskell environment.

Aside from Vitalik, there's also the Ethereum Foundation, a non-profit dedicated to supporting Ethereum and related technologies, the Ethereum Enterprise Alliance (EEA), a member-led industry collective aiming to empower organizations to adopt + use Ethereum technology in their day-to-day business operations, as well as Consensys, the dedicated Ethereum software development firm behind products like MetaMask, Quorum & Infura. On the grassroots development side of things, you'll find numerous hackathons & coding summits geared to attract talent into the space. Everywhere you look, there are dozens upon dozens of unique entities that have emerged intent on driving the Ethereum ecosystem forward.

Blockchain's Largest Development Community Due to the composability inherent within Ethereum's coding language & the limited programmability of Bitcoin, most of the development throughout the blockchain & digital asset sector involves Ethereum. No doubt, it should be expected that Bitcoin will see more & more development over time. Whereas Bitcoin mainly exists to preserve & store value, Ethereum is the go-to choice for *powering* blockchain native applications, services & products.

An Ambitious Nature Since inception the Ethereum protocol & its community have been quite audacious, proclaiming massive goals that may seem like a lot to bite off, perhaps even *too* much so. Perhaps the most striking example of such ambition is the planned merger of the current Ethereum blockchain with the ETH2.0 beacon chain. The London upgrade posed a similar challenge & yet, was executed relatively smoothly. Only time will tell how things will play out down the road as matters become more technically complex.

A Collaborative Spirit Whether Satoshi Nakamoto was a single entity or thousands of individuals, there's been very little in the way of substantial development, changes, or additions to the Bitcoin protocol since it was initially deployed to the mainnet. In all fairness, upgradability was never the real goal for Bitcoin, launching with most of its pure intent already fully realized, technologically speaking. For Ethereum, things have basically been the exact opposite, where the goal has been to continue pushing forward & building. Thus far the principles have been quite clear: so long as the application being designed, developed or built truly benefits from native blockchain integration - there always seems to be a member within the community ready to pitch in & help bring the idea to fruition.

Talent Specialization The blockchain & digital asset industry is rife with sub-sectors, each sub-sector housing various niches. Inside the DeFi scene alone you have self-custody wallets, payment apps, high yield saving protocols, staking protocols, prediction markets, data aggregators - the list goes on & on. It can't be overstated how many distinct niches already exist with more emerging all the time. Such growth inside of this tech-centric field encourages high specialization amongst participants hoping to make a name for themselves. Similarly, if you hope to maximize your ROI in the space, I'd recommend you also develop an investment "specialty". Some people are drawn towards DeFi opportunities, others are drawn to NFTs, some focus on gaming. The choice is yours.

Weaknesses Of Ethereum's Team

Move Fast & Break Things A commonly, perhaps overly used, axiom inside the tech & investing world is "Move fast. Break things." This mindset has certainly been infused into the DNA of the Ethereum development community. The result? Sometimes things *actually* break. The good news? It's not often the Ethereum network itself or the underlying Ethereum code breaks. It's typically an issue with a smart contract's composition or execution or some other piece of infrastructure supporting the protocol that experiences problems.

Prominent Leader There's a sizable cohort within the blockchain + cryptocurrency space who are committed to the sector for more than the technology. For many it's the ethos, the spirit, the philosophy of trustlessness + confirmed verifiability that tempts them in. With that "trustless" principle in mind, the idea of having a leader is off-putting to many as it directly opposes their underlying value of decentralization. On one hand, prominent leaders like Vitalik can be pivotal in keeping a distributed project like Ethereum focused & mindful of the road ahead. If that leadership is used maliciously or otherwise diverts the project away from its intentions & stated goals though, it can become a problem.

Diffused Efforts A key benefit of a project like Bitcoin is that developers are usually working on the same thing to solve a clear issue. This is possible because of Bitcoin's focused mission. With so many subcategories + niches emerging from Ethereum over the years, developers are spread out across the various projects nested within the network's ecosystem. Instead of everybody rallying to coordinate + laser focus their energy on a specific aspect of the greater protocol, a ton of talent gets diffused + distributed.

Ethereum Economics: *Tokenomics*

The Bullish Case For Ethereum

Staked Tokens Exiting Circulation When investors stake their coins, whether directly on the network with a minimum of 32+ ETH or contributing to a larger pool - coins are removed from circulation. As more coins are removed from circulation there tends to be a positive upward effect on the price of Ethereum. This bullish impact stems from basic supply/demand economics. As supply decreases scarcity increases. As scarcity increases the demand of the coin increases. As demand increases, the perceived value follows suit.

Gas Powered dApps Though most blockchains use their native coins to pay for fees, Ethereum is unrivaled when it comes to the volume of transactions on its network. The prevalence of smart contracts underpinning DEXs, liquidity pools, yield farms, NFTs, & other dApps gives ETH substantial real-world utility. Regardless of one's preference for ETH as an investment, many will still find themselves purchasing ETH because they *have* to, thus reinforcing the demand side pressure for the asset & positively impacting its price.

EIP-1559's Burn Mechanism Though the London Upgrade contained additional improvements, EIP-1559's restructuring of fee auctions is likely to have a positive effect on the price of Ethereum. The new change means gas spent during transactions is burned, effectively removing ETH from the circulating supply. Supply + demand economics strikes again!

Triple Point Asset Assets come in various forms. In short, you have capital assets, consumable assets, & store of value assets. Suffice it to say, Ethereum serves as all three classes, something that is quite rare for any asset, digital or otherwise. While more & more smart contract platforms are positioning themselves to claim "Triple Point" status, Ethereum is the current leader by far, having done the most to prove itself viable of all three categories. We shall explore this "Triple Point" concept in more depth later.

The Bearish Case For Ethereum

Mutable Monetary Policy Historically, Ethereum has been everchanging in its pursuit of creating the "open internet". Embedded in its ethos & plainly stated in the white paper is a philosophical commitment to be agile + nimble. This means the core dev team will alter or otherwise change plans so long as it moves the protocol towards realizing its greater ambitions. This mutability makes some a bit wary though.

The most pressing concern is typically the realization that unlike Bitcoin, the design + functionality of ETH's tokenomics can be altered at any moment. In the case of EIP-1559, the alteration may benefit the asset's price. Nevertheless, it must be understood that not every change to the protocol will prove favorable. Point in case being the major consensus bug that affected over half of all nodes running Geth, the most widely used Ethereum node software client, resulting in a chain split. The issue stemmed from a vulnerability within Geth that was quickly patched. Nevertheless, given the event happened within weeks of the London upgrade, I would wager that Ethereum's "nimble" nature may be at fault.

Unlimited Supply Even though EIP-1559 introduced some additional positive price pressure by removing ETH from circulation, there's still an unlimited supply with no fixed cap on new issuance. Compared against Bitcoin's 21M hard ca, ETH's appreciation potential is constrained by its free-flowing supply policy.

Ethereum's Ambitious Intentions

Ethereum has been a complex + ambitious project since day 1. Where Bitcoin laid out a concise and singular purpose, Ethereum cast a vision of an entire ecosystem that could emerge from its Turing-complete code base. While Bitcoin launched in near "final form", Ethereum debuted pursuing a new frontier of internet-enabled computing and applications.

Extrapolating upon the promise of smart contracts + dApps, possibilities detailed at inception included tokenization systems, financial derivatives, stable currency pegs, DAOs, prediction markets + more. Though it has endured technical hurdles & many remain to be cleared, Ethereum has already realized many of its intentions. Housing more development + evolution than any other blockchain project in history, it appears ETH2.0 will continue pressing forward towards the horizon to chart new territories. Ethereum is the internet's future.

"

Unless you are breaking stuff, you aren't moving fast enough

"

Mark Zuckerberg

Ethereum's Resilience Through Time

Wanton Development: *Ambition + Prudence Collide*

A philosophical tenet spelled out in the white paper; "agility" means Ethereum is open to changes & adjustments so long as they help manifest the protocol's greater ambitions. An arduous roadmap paired with constant changes may lead to unintended consequences or create vulnerabilities. Most exploits are not due to errors in Ethereum's underlying code, but rather to improperly composed or poorly coded smart contracts.

Breaking Things: *Moving Too Fast*

Ethereum's technical complexities require changes to be deployed in stages rather than in one major update. This iterative approach in unison with its composability means more opportunities for flawed code to be exploited by bad actors. The DAO hack that led to the Ethereum Classic (ETC) hard fork is the most significant breach to directly impact Ethereum's protocol layer. Most exploits only affect specific smart contracts, not Ethereum's base layer.

The first decentralized autonomous organization & one of Ethereum's earliest crowdfunded projects when it launched back in 2016, The DAO collected over $150M worth of ETH from its token sale. Shortly after launching a vulnerability was discovered & exploited to the tune of more than $60M worth of ETH.

This immense loss of funds forced Ethereum's leadership to decide how to handle the incident, the crypto purist approach being to let the hack stand. If the central goal of the blockchain is to act as an immutable ledger, the ledger should remain unmuted + free from intervention. Otherwise, the fundamentally "decentralized" nature of the Ethereum ledger would become questionable.

Ultimately, Vitalik wound up proposing a soft fork for the network, adding a piece of code that blacklisted the attacker, effectively preventing them from moving the stolen funds. To implement this solution the team had to force a split from the main Ethereum chain via hard fork so that they could roll back the chain to its prior pre-hack state.

Obviously, not all were happy about this route. Many would have preferred to lose their funds & maintain the "trustless" integrity of Ethereum. The users who opposed the rollback pressed forward with the original hacked chain, refusing to migrate to the new fork. This saga is the reason for why there's two Ethereum projects, "Ethereum" (ETH) & "Ethereum Classic "(ETC). Though ETC is indeed the original + unaltered

Ethereum chain, most users + developers migrated over to the new Ethereum, which is the network that most are referring to when they mention ETH or Ethereum.

Scaling Issues: *Network Congestion*

While a positive metric of adoption, the growing usage of dApps puts a technical strain on the Ethereum network‘s low throughput. A sign of things to come, “Crypto Kitties” foreshadowed the effects of congestion exposed during 2020’s DeFi summer. Failed transactions created a punishing environment for novices looking to explore trustless capital markets, meanwhile surging gas fees made DeFi trading, yield farming + minting NFTs unprofitable for most users.

Funny enough, a very similar issue occurred in 2021, not because of DeFi but due to the NFT usage. As NFT's sizzled down after their initial Q1 boom it was meme coins like Shiba Inu’s SHIB, Safemoon’s SAFE, & CumRocket’s CUMMIES that drove gas prices through the roof as many a degenerate rushed to their nearest DEX in attempt to ride the latest wave.

All this surging interest would otherwise be quite welcome if not for the negative feedback loop. High usage leads to network congestion which causes ludicrous gas fees that force most smaller users trading with meager accounts out of the market as the transaction cost erode what may have been an otherwise profitable play.

It's not all doom-and-gloom though. New scaling solutions are constantly being developed and deployed to help ease the burden on Ethereum's base layer. Around Q2 2021 Polygon launched their side-chain solution which led to the explosion of their MATIC token, growing by over 10X in less than 90 days. More recently Arbitrum debuted their main net, allowing users to trade with lower fees, too. We're also seeing other remedies like Starkware power the gasless Layer 2 version of decentralized leverage trading platform dYdX.

Maximum Extractable Value: *Front Runners FTW*

MEV, sometimes referred to as *miner* extractable value, is an issue of front-running bots exploiting Ethereum to siphon value from the network in the form of inflated fees. The "Flash Boys" research study from Cornell was the first academic paper to address the issue, conveying the complex risks created by transaction-ordering dependencies inherent within smart contracts. Not dissimilar to Wall Street HFT (high frequency trading) techniques, miners deploy arbitrage bots to bid up the average gas price via Priority Gas Auctions (PGAs), influencing the prioritization of transactions being added to the block in order to drain profits from the network. MistX is a DEX specifically created to minimize MEV.

MEV was theorized in the early days of Ethereum, but it didn't become a legitimate issue until network activity began to surge from the bubbling bull market of 2020 and 2021. Thankfully for Ethereum's robust developer community there are already tools being created + deployed to help minimize this issue, such as the aforementioned DEX, MistX, an enhanced Uniswap architected + optimized to minimize the potential for any MEV-related fees from impacting users. For those interested, I'd recommend checking out Sandwiched.WTF, another platform created by the same developers of MistX. Sandwiched allows users to scan their wallets to see how affected they may have been by the MEV problem. Just connect your wallet or into an address & viola.

"

When decentralized blockchain protocols start displacing centralized web services, we'll start to see real internet-based sovereignty. The future internet will be decentralized.

"

Olaf Carlson-Wee

Why Ethereum Is Thriving

Growing Adoption: *ETH Eats The World... Wide Web*

"Bitcoin not blockchain" was a common expression back when most projects were technically vaporware. Smart contracts have turned the tide. Today, most top projects have launched their core offerings + established product market fit. From DEXs like Uniswap + Raydium to savings + borrowing protocols like AAVE + Anchor, most valuable projects are dApps built atop Ethereum + powered by ETH.

Decentralized Finance: *Trustless Markets*

Peer-to-peer financial applications have brought many users to Ethereum. The composability of smart contracts simplifies + speeds up the build process for developers looking to quickly execute their ideas. Platforms like Aave + Compound entice with passive income + leverage, while DEXs like Uniswap provide users with private, discrete trading. For a summary of the various DeFi protocols & to see how they are performing in terms of volume or total value locked (TVL), be sure to check out DeFi Llama or DeFi Pulse.

Non-Fungible Tokens: *Verifiable Legitimacy*

Some like Gary V believe Ethereum's killer app isn't DeFi but instead NFTs. Like 2020's DeFi summer, 2021 saw NFT adoption go parabolic as Christie's auctioned Beeple's "The First 5000 Days" for $69M + Jay-Z sold "Reasonable Doubt" via Sotheby's virtual Decentraland branch. Beneath the speculation, NFTs are crucial for bridging physical + digital assets, providing verifiable legitimacy on the blockchain.

Beeple's $69 NFT auction with Christie's was a definitive moment for many, me included. That single event vindicated the nascent space in a way that couldn't be undone or go unrecognized. It was the proverbial bell that can't be unrung. Following Beeple's meteoric Q1 ascent, Jay-Z partnered with Sotheby's to auction his album "Reasonable Doubt" as an NFT. Not to be undone by Christie's, the collaborative pair hosted + conducted the auction inside a virtual Sotheby's housed within the Voltaire art district of the Metaverse, Decentraland's blockchain-based virtual world.

This is virtual pivot is such a powerful move because it shows that legacy institutions like Sotheby's & Christie's aren't blindly focused on the money-making potential of NFTs, but are sufficiently enthused to go a step further to truly embrace the new possibilities of art's latest medium. Even if profits were the only motive, it would still add legitimacy & visibility for the industry, a net positive. Nevertheless, it's a lovely thing to see such titans of the legacy world adapt to become full-fledged participants of what's happening within the blockchain ecosystem.

Institutional Adoption: *Smart Money*

Ethereum is getting more attention than ever as a valuable asset in the eyes and minds of large investment firms + institutions. Whether it's JPMorgan building Quorum, a permissioned Ethereum fork or Goldman Sachs offering their clients ETH products, the smart money is investing time, resources + talent towards ETH and the broader Ethereum ecosystem.

For years different institutions, banks, & money managers have been eyeing the blockchain evolution from the sidelines, cautiously awaiting the next major wave of adoption to justify their entry into the space. In the interim they've built out research teams, hired engineers, & forged alliances with digital asset companies to improve their vantage of the sector. Between the efforts of organizations like the Ethereum Enterprise Alliance (EEA) & New York Digital Investment Group (NYDIG), legacy incumbents are recognizing they must adapt to the blockchain future if they hope to remain relevant. At this stage of the game the actions & moves being made are long term oriented, not seasonal changes that wither away once the bull run cools down. With decades of storied histories, even centuries old legacies in some cases, the institutional adoption of digital assets and blockchain technology is only beginning.

"

Blockchain technology has such a wide range of transformational use cases, from recreating the plumbing of Wall Street to creating financial sovereignty in the farthest regions of the world.

"

Perianne Boring

Why Ethereum Will Prosper

Tailwinds For Ethereum's Growth

Swift iteration to realize an ambitious vision has fueled the rapid development + adoption of Ethereum. With so many real-world use cases inspiring the creation of countless products, services + companies revolving around dApps + smart contracts, Ethereum is the most valuable + impactful blockchain ecosystem.

Triple Point Asset Thesis: *The Economic Trifecta*

The most successful investors have a propensity to concentrate on a specific type of instrument or vehicle within the market. Regardless, the instrument of choice will fall into one asset class or another. Though there is no universally accepted list of distinct asset classes, we'll reference David Hoffman's tripart categorization as I find it a simple yet inclusive model defining all investments as either capital assets, consumable assets, or store of value assets.

Capital assets are characterized by generating an ongoing source of net present value versus expected future returns. In the category of capital assets are equities, bonds, and income producing real estate. Each has its own value & its own cohort of participants interested in capital assets because of their inherent cashflow qualities. While this class is likely to produce the highest returns, it also poses the greatest downside risk.

Next up: consumable assets. Often viewed as commodities, this class can be consumed or transformed into another asset bearing economic value. Sitting in the middle of the road of profitability & risk, this group is fairly price stable compared to capital assets. Muted downward price pressure & a lack of ongoing yield reveals the need for conversion to access any underlying value. Grains, oil, timber, rare earth metals, cotton + hemp are all examples of consumable assets.

This brings us to store of value assets. These assets cannot be consumed, nor do they generate ongoing income. Nevertheless, the ability to store & preserve value on macro time frames is their greatest trait. Gold, diamonds, productive farmland + fine art are all examples of SoV assets. Plenty of economist would suggest currency to be a SoV, but most still in existence are no more than baseless fiat depreciating at alarming rates, so I won't cosign that preposterous idea. A better SoV to currency would be firearms + ammunition.

Carrying each of the three distinct class qualities, ETH serves as a capital asset when staked or leveraged as collateral, a consumable good when burned as gas & as a store of value for long-term holders. As each of ETH's sub-utilities gain adoption + usage, its value is likely to increase in a virtuous cycle.

Programmable Money: *Stablecoins & CBDCs*

Fiat-stable token pegs have proven their utility + value within the blockchain ecosystem to escape volatility + earn high yield with low risk. Further, the concept of programmable money has attracted many countries + governments looking to issue their own digital currencies. These coins can be centralized like Circle's USDC or fully trustless like Maker's DAI.

There were no stable coins when Bitcoin launched. If you wanted to dive into crypto you had to expose yourself to immense volatility. Well, stablecoins take care of that. Add in yield rates many orders of magnitude greater than what most investors + consumers can access with their bank's "high yield" savings account (often a paltry 0.2% -0.4%) & digital asset use because much more attractive. Platforms like Nexo & BlockFi can easily generate risk free yields between 3% & 8% that compound daily should you choose to earn in stablecoins opposed to volatile assets like ETH or DOT.

Programmable money is revolutionary. Up to this point in modern recorded history, there's never been a way for the issuer of a currency to influence how the currency behaves, collect data on the how the currency is being used & audit users - all in real time. This system, though not 100% accurate as some oracles lag others & savvy users leverage bots to spoof data to preserve their privacy, it is far closer to being accurate than anything else that's come before.

Programmable money creates an abundance of opportunities: dynamic interest rates, preferred vendors, targeted fund disbursements, real-time credit assessments. Programmable money creates an abundance of risk: *dynamic* interest rates, *preferred* vendors, *targeted* fund disbursements, real-time credit *assessments*. (No, that's not a typo.)

It may be difficult to comprehend the gravity of a centrally controlled digital currency, but I urge you to reminisce on the days before iPhones + Facebook were ubiquitous, before candid conversations were recorded + turned into tailored ads targeting your unique data set in elaborately evolving algorithms designed to monetize every iota of your soul. What would happen if that same degree of control via surveillance + suggestion was ported directly to your wallet?

Consider China's digital Yuan. Just like a blockchain, this digitally native version of the currency allows the state to monitor everything on the Yuan ledger. Operators can see exactly how funds are being used, where they're being spent, & how somebody received their funds. In some instances, like solving a crime, these are useful features. On the contrary, such granular control over a centralized currency could be used to victimize individuals who oppose or defy the edicts, decrees + desires of the state by freezing funds. Further, this system could allow the dissident's wallet address to be "blacklisted", not just preventing any withdrawals or deposits from being made but going so far as to punish any other address that even *attempts* to interact with the blacklisted account.

For all the benefits digital assets bring, this is the stark road ahead that we must prepare for. If we don't begin to have honest, raw dialogues about the risks of this new global system now, it'll be too late before we even realize it.

The Great Talent Transfer: *Brain Drain*

The blockchain industry has attracted the world's top talent at an accelerating rate over the past decade. The influx of minds brings fresh capital in tow, helping create jobs in the process. In many ways, Ethereum's dApp ecosystem is the new Silicon Valley. From Silk Road prosecutor Katie Huan joining Coinbase's board to former Apple executive Todd Brooks heading to Ledger, & even former US Comptroller of Currency Brian Brooks' stint as the CEO of Binance.US, more people than ever are opting to make blockchain + crypto their top priority.

History has shown us time & again that when highly qualified, highly compensated experts like begin leaving their fields en masse to pivot towards a burgeoning industry, it's a leading indicator of that fields impending boom. Why else would such specialist forfeit their secured roles to bet on an "unproven' sector? Do they know something the general public doesn't? Are they leveraging their asymmetric information to front run the growth opportunity? Why such intense conviction? I make no claims to have the precise answer. Just know - the blockchain + digital asset driven talent transfer is not something to scoff at in the slightest.

"

The blockchain cannot be described just as a revolution. It's a tsunami-like phenomena, slowly advancing and gradually enveloping everything along its way by the force of its progression.

"

William Movia

Recommended Resources

Exchanges

https://www.coinbase.com/

https://www.kraken.com/

https://www.gemini.com/

https://www.kucoin.com/

https://uniswap.org/

https://www.sushi.com/

https://1inch.io/

https://dydx.exchange/

https://www.perp.fi/

https://www.swanbitcoin.com/

Wallets

https://ethereum.org/en/wallets/

https://metamask.io/

https://www.exodus.com/

https://www.ledger.com/

https://trezor.io/

Crypto Debit + Credit Cards

https://bitpay.com/

https://nexo.io/nexo-card

https://crypto.com/cards

https://www.gemini.com/credit-card/waitlist

https://blockfi.com/

https://nexo.io/

Borrowing + Lending Protocols

https://aave.com/

https://compound.finance/

https://oasis.app/borrow

https://app.anchorprotocol.com/earn

https://homora.alphafinance.io/

The History Of Banking

https://www.imf.org/en/About

https://www.worldbank.org/en/who-we-are

https://www.bis.org/

Research Tools

https://coinmarketcap.com/

https://www.coingecko.com/en

https://glassnode.com/

https://www.chainalysis.com/

https://dune.xyz/home

https://defipulse.com/

https://defillama.com/home

Cited Works

Adams, Derrick. "An NFT in Celebration of JAY-Z's Reasonable Doubt 25th Anniversary." *Sothebys.com*, www.sothebys.com/en/digital-catalogues/heir-to-the-throne.

Amadeo, Kimberly. "Top 10 Economic Predictions for the Next 10 Years." Edited by Somer Anderson, *The Balance*, 27 Aug. 2021, www.thebalance.com/top-economic-predictions-for-the-next-10-years-3305699.

The Austrian Investor. "Keyesian Economics vs Austrian Economics." *Cdn.thinglink.me*, cdn.thinglink.me/api/image/642450897460264961/1024/10/scaletowidth/0/0/1/1/false/true?wait=true.

Bachman, and I Capulet. "Digital Record of Tesla Crashes Resulting in Death." *TeslaDeaths.com*, Tesla Deaths, 15 Sept. 2021, www.tesladeaths.com/.

Beigel, Ofir. "What Is Bitcoin? A Complete Beginner's Guide." *99 Bitcoins*, 13 Jan. 2021, 99bitcoins.com/bitcoin/#what_is_bitcoin.

Bitcoin Insider. “Ethereum Gas Fees Surge to All-Time High on Meme Coin Pumps.” *Bitcoin Insider*, 12 May 2021, www.bitcoininsider.org/article/113436/ethereum-gas-fees-surge-all-time-high-meme-coin-pumps.

Bitcoin.org. “Running A Full Node.” *Bitcoin*, bitcoin.org/en/full-node#what-is-a-full-node.

Buterin, Vitalik. “Ethereum Whitepaper.” *Ethereum.org*, 2013, ethereum.by/en/whitepaper/#philosophy.

Chainlink. “DeFi Yield Farming Explained.” *Chainlink Blog*, SmartContract Chainlink Ltd SEZC, 14 Oct. 2020, blog.chain.link/defi-yield-farming-explained/.

Chainlink. “What Is Miner-Extractable Value (MEV)?” *Chainlink Blog*, SmartContract Chainlink Ltd SEZC, 10 Mar. 2021, blog.chain.link/what-is-miner-extractable-value-mev/.

Chen, James. “Bretton Woods Agreement and System: An Overview.” Edited by Somer Anderson, *Investopedia*, Investopedia, 28 Apr. 2021, www.investopedia.com/terms/b/brettonwoodsagreement.asp.

Chen, James. “What You Should Know About Petrodollars.” Edited by Gordon Scott, *Investopedia*, Investopedia, 10 May 2021, www.investopedia.com/terms/p/petrodollars.asp.

Chipolina, Scott, and Matt Hussey. “What Are Dapps?” *Decrypt*, Decrypt, 1 Oct. 2020, decrypt.co/resources/dapps.

Christie's. “Beeple's Opus.” *Beeple: A Visionary Digital Artist at the Forefront of NFTs | Christie's*, Christies, 11 Mar. 2021, www.christies.com/features/Monumental-collage-by-Beeple-is-first-purely-digital-artwork-NFT-to-come-to-auction-11510-7.aspx.

Coinbase. “What Is DeFi?” *Coinbase*, Coinbase, 2021, www.coinbase.com/learn/crypto-basics/what-is-defi.

Copeland, Tim. “The Complete Story of the QuadrigaCX $190 Million Scandal.” *Decrypt*, Decrypt, 13 Mar. 2019, decrypt.co/5853/complete-story-quadrigacx-190-million.

Coverdale, Chris. “A Beginner’s Guide: Private and Public Key Cryptography Deciphered.” *Medium*, 26 Feb. 2018, medium.com/coinmonks/private-and-public-key-cryptography-explained-simply-4c374d371736.

Crawley, Jamie. "Elizabeth Warren Gives SEC July 28 Deadline to Figure Out Crypto Regulation." *Nasdaq*, 8 July 2021, www.nasdaq.com/articles/elizabeth-warren-gives-sec-july-28-deadline-to-figure-out-crypto-regulation-2021-07-08.

Cryptopedia Staff. "What Was The DAO?" *Gemini*, 27 Apr. 2021, www.gemini.com/cryptopedia/the-dao-hack-makerdao.

Daian, Philip et al. "Flash Boys 2.0: Frontrunning, Transaction Reordering, and Consensus Instability in Decentralized Exchanges." ArXiv abs/1904.05234 (2019): n. pag.

Dans, Enrique. "Bitcoin And Latin American Economies: Danger Or Opportunity?" *Forbes*, Forbes Magazine, 28 June 2021, www.forbes.com/sites/enriquedans/2021/06/14/bitcoin-and-latin-american-economies-danger-or-opportunity/?sh=4251af905bfe.

Data Lab. "Federal Response to COVID-19 ." *Datalab.usaspending.gov*, U.S. Treasury Data Lab, datalab.usaspending.gov/federal-covid-funding/.

De, Nikhilesh. "State of Crypto: Federal Regulations Are Coming Into Focus." *CoinDesk*, Digital Currency Group, 1 June 2021, 9:30 AM, www.coindesk.com/biden-administration-crypto-regulation-hints.

Dicamillo, Nate. "Coinbase Debuts Savings Product with 4% APY on USDC DEPOSITS." *Nasdaq*, 29 June 2021, 10:30 AM, www.nasdaq.com/articles/coinbase-debuts-savings-product-with-4-apy-on-usdc-deposits-2021-06-29.

Dirham, Dinarh. "The Rise and Fall of Fiat Currencies." *Dinar Dirham*, 12 Oct. 2018, www.dinardirham.com/the-rise-and-fall-of-fiat-currencies/.

"Ethereum Wallets." *Ethereum.org*, ethereum.org/en/wallets/.

Ethereum.org. "Decentralized Applications (Dapps)." *Ethereum.org*, ethereum.org/en/dapps/#what-are-dapps.

Ethereum.org. "Introduction to Smart Contracts." *Ethereum.org*, ethereum.org/nb/developers/docs/smart-contracts/.

Ethereum.org. "What Is Proof-Of-Stake (POS)?" *Ethereum.org*, ethereum.org/en/developers/docs/consensus-mechanisms/pos/#what-is-pos.

“Federal Reserve Actions to Support the Flow of Credit to Households and Businesses.” *FederalReserve.Gov*, Board of Governors of the Federal Reserve System, 15 Mar. 2020, www.federalreserve.gov/newsevents/pressreleases/monetary20200315b.htm.

“Final Rule: Amending the ‘Accredited Investor’ Definition.” *SEC.gov*, U.S. Securities and Exchange Commission, 26 Aug. 2020, www.sec.gov/rules/final/2020/33-10824.pdf.

Frost, Liam. “'I Felt like a Moron' for Not Buying Bitcoin, SAYS Billionaire STANLEY DRUCKENMILLER.” *CryptoSlate*, 30 May 2021, cryptoslate.com/i-felt-like-a-moron-for-not-buying-bitcoin-says-billionaire-stanley-druckenmiller/.

“Gavin Wood.” *Gavin Wood*, gavwood.com/.

Hayes, Adam. “What Happens to Bitcoin After All 21 Million Are Mined?” Edited by Khadija Khartit, *Investopedia*, Investopedia, 28 Feb. 2021, www.investopedia.com/tech/what-happens-bitcoin-after-21-million-mined/.

Heakal, Reem. "What Is the Bank for International Settlements?" Edited by Margaret James, *Investopedia*, Investopedia, 17 Sept. 2021, www.investopedia.com/articles/03/120903.asp.

Hoffman, David. "Bankless." 4 Oct. 2019.

"Home." *Ethereum Foundation*, ethereum.foundation/.

"How Does Bitcoin Work?" *Bitcoin*, bitcoin.org/en/how-it-works.

"How Does Bitcoin Work?" *Bitcoin*, bitcoin.org/en/how-it-works.

How Money Works, director. *Is The World Bank Actually an Evil Empire? - How Money Works*, How Money Works, 5 Mar. 2021, www.youtube.com/watch?v=BKZGk0DN1Mg&ab_channel=HowMoneyWorks.

Ibañez, Juan Ignacio and Bayer, Chris N. and Tasca, Paolo and Xu, Jiahua, REA, Triple-Entry Accounting and Blockchain: Converging Paths to Shared Ledger Systems (May 15, 2020). Available at SSRN: Ibañez, Juan Ignacio and Bayer, Chris N. and Tasca, Paolo and Xu, Jiahua, REA, Triple-Entry Accounting and Blockchain: Converging Paths to Shared Ledger Systems (May 15,

2020). Available at SSRN:
https://ssrn.com/abstract=3602207

IOHK. "Programming Languages." *Cardano Testnets*, IOHK, testnets.cardano.org/en/programming-languages/plutus/overview/.

James, Ryan. "FTX Partners With MLB to Further Expand Crypto Awareness." *Yahoo! Finance*, Yahoo!, 23 June 2021, finance.yahoo.com/news/ftx-partners-mlb-further-expand-143000516.html.

Kelly, Jack. "Cryptocurrency Companies Are Waging A War For Talent In A Hot Job Market." *Forbes*, Forbes Magazine, 26 June 2021, 1:19 PM, www.forbes.com/sites/jackkelly/2021/06/26/cryptocurrency-companies-waging-a--a-war-for-talent-in-a-hot-job-market/?sh=44ed34416b19.

Lee, Isabelle. "Argo Blockchain and DMG Look to Mint First-Ever 'GREEN Bitcoin' with Launch of Clean Energy Mining Operation." *Business Insider*, Business Insider, 26 Mar. 2021, 12:12 PM, markets.businessinsider.com/currencies/news/bitcoin-argo-blockchain-and-dmg-to-mint-ever-green-btc-2021-3.

Lewitinn, Lawrence. “Hedge Fund Billionaire Ray Dalio: ‘I Have Some Bitcoin.’” *CoinDesk*, Digital Currency Group, 24 May 2021, www.coindesk.com/consensus-ray-dalio-i-have-some-bitcoin.

Magazine, Bitcoin. “Interview: Mass Bitcoin Adoption in Latin America.” *Bitcoin Magazine: Bitcoin News, Articles, Charts, and Guides*, Bitcoin Magazine: Bitcoin News, Articles, Charts, and Guides, 24 June 2021, bitcoinmagazine.com/business/mass-bitcoin-adoption-in-latin-america.

Marinoff, Nick. “Cynthia Lummis: Retirees Should Diversify with Crypto.” *Live Bitcoin News*, 2 July 2021, 3:00 PM, www.livebitcoinnews.com/cynthia-lummis-retirees-should-diversify-with-crypto/.

Mason, Emily. “JPMorgan Says Ethereum Upgrades Could Jumpstart $40 Billion Staking Industry.” *Forbes*, Forbes Magazine, 1 July 2021, www.forbes.com/sites/emilymason/2021/07/01/jpmorgan-says-ethereum-upgrades-could-jumpstart-40-billion-staking-industry/?sh=4f9a44415128.

MassMutual. "Institutional Bitcoin Provider NYDIG Announces Minority STAKE Purchase by Massmutual." *MassMutual.com*, Massachusetts Mutual Life Insurance Company, 10 Dec. 2020, www.massmutual.com/about-us/news-and-press-releases/press-releases/2020/12/institutional-bitcoin-provider-nydig-announces-minority-stake-purchase-by-massmutual.

Maverick, J.B. "International Monetary Fund (IMF) vs. the World Bank: What's the Difference?" Edited by Katrina Munichiello, *Investopedia*, Investopedia, 30 Sept. 2020, www.investopedia.com/ask/answers/043015/what-difference-between-international-monetary-fund-and-world-bank.asp.

McMillan, Robert. "The Inside Story of Mt. Gox, Bitcoin's $460 Million Disaster." *Wired*, Conde Nast, 3 Mar. 2014, www.wired.com/2014/03/bitcoin-exchange/.

MIT OpenCourseWare. "Blockchain & Money." *MIT.edu*, MIT, ocw.mit.edu/courses/sloan-school-of-management/15-

s12-blockchain-and-money-fall-2018/lecture-slides/MIT15_S12F18_ses4.pdf.

Nakamoto, Satoshi. “Bitcoin: A Peer-to-Peer Electronic Cash System.” Bitcoin.org, Oct. 2008.

One Minute Economics, director. *The Bretton Woods Monetary System (1944 - 1971) Explained in One Minute*, One Minute Economics, 10 Jan. 2017, www.youtube.com/watch?v=RtFz9q26t5A&ab_channel=OneMinuteEconomics.

One Minute Economics, director. *The International Monetary Fund (IMF) and the World Bank Explained in One Minute*, One Minute Economics, 16 July 2016, www.youtube.com/watch?v=WG72yk60tbA&ab_channel=OneMinuteEconomics.

One Minute Economics, director. *Three Types of Money in One Minute: Commodity Money, Representative Money and Fiat Money*/Currency*, One Minute Economics, 20 Oct. 2018, www.youtube.com/watch?v=_HR7ocy6eAE.

O'Sullivan, Andrea. “Is El Salvador's Embrace of Bitcoin Good, Bad, or Both?” *Reason.com*, Reason, 6 July 2021, reason.com/2021/07/06/is-el-salvadors-embrace-of-bitcoin-good-bad-or-both/.

Pires, Francisco. “Ethereum Blockchain Was Split Over Outdated Geth Software Nodes.” *Tom's Hardware*, Tom's Hardware, 31 Aug. 2021, www.tomshardware.com/news/ethereum-blockchain-split-geth.

Rana, Kapil. “Triple Entry Accounting System: A Revolution With Blockchain.” *Medium*, DataSeries, 26 Mar. 2020, medium.com/dataseries/triple-entry-accounting-system-a-revolution-with-blockchain-768f4d8cabd8.

Reynolds, Sam. “Bug in Ethereum Interface Causes Inadvertent Chain Split, Chaos on Network.” *Blockworks*, 27 Aug. 2021, blockworks.co/bug-in-ethereum-interface-causes-inadvertent-chain-split-chaos-on-network/.

Reynolds, Sam. “Ether Burns Hit $100 Million Post EIP-1559 Activation.” *Blockworks*, 11 Aug. 2021, blockworks.co/ether-burns-hit-100-million-post-eip-1559-activation/.

Roberts, Daniel. “FTX CEO on 19-Year Miami Heat Sponsorship: 'We Don't Need the Other 18 Years to Have the Funds'.” *Decrypt*, Decrypt, 7 May 2021, decrypt.co/70004/ftx-ceo-sbf-19-year-miami-heat-stadium-deal-funds.

“SEC Modernizes the Accredited Investor Definition.” *SEC.Gov*, U.S. Securities and Exchange Commission, 26 Aug. 2020, www.sec.gov/news/press-release/2020-191.

Sharma, Rakesh. “Decentralized Finance (Defi) Definition and Use Cases.” *Investopedia*, Investopedia, 14 Mar. 2021, www.investopedia.com/decentralized-finance-defi-5113835.

Sinclair, Sebastian. “Bitcoin Mining Council Says Sustainable Power Mix on the Rise.” *CoinDesk*, Digital Currency Group, 2 July 2021, www.coindesk.com/bitcoin-mining-council-sustainable-power-mix-survey-crypto.

Tarud , Jonathan. “Decentralized Applications (DApps) Explained.” *Koombea*, 22 Apr. 2021, www.koombea.com/blog/decentralized-applications-dapps-explained/.

Team, The Investopedia. “What Is Money?” Edited by Robert C Kelly, *Investopedia*, Investopedia, 22 June 2021, www.investopedia.com/insights/what-is-money/.

Team, The Investopedia. “What Is Money?” *Investopedia*, Investopedia, 22 June 2021, www.investopedia.com/insights/what-is-money/.

TheInfographicsShow, The Inforgraphics Show, director. *How Petrodollars Affect The US Dollar And The World Economy?*, The Infographics Show, 14 Dec. 2018, www.youtube.com/watch?v=-XU6ZHZ8TDg.

The World Bank. *World Bank Group Annual Reports 2020*, The World Bank, 2020, thedocs.worldbank.org/en/doc/832891604352590592-0090022020/original/WorldBankGroupAnnualReportsExecutiveSummary.pdf.

Yao, Siqiu, et al. “The Byzantine General's Problem.” Cornell Courses: Distributed Systems. 2018.

ZeroCap. “Why Ether Is Superior: The Triple Point Asset.” *Zerocap*, 20 Aug. 2021, zerocap.com/why-ether-is-superior/.

About The Author

Sae'Von Springer is the founder & managing partner of Native Assets, a blockchain firm specializing in empowering clients with the knowledge & tools required to secure their assets, preserve their purchasing power, & compound their wealth via conscious implementation of blockchain technologies & strategically leveraged digital asset markets. The once Ivy-League bound scholar & athlete turned rapper/producer + cannabis entrepreneur is perhaps the least likely candidate to have founded the industry's premier blockchain education + certification program.

"

I grew up on food stamps sleeping on the floor with drug addicts living in the attic. I only say that to make the point that I know what it's like to lack proper financial wisdom & guidance.

Financial security, let alone wealth, just wasn't the norm in my community. Instead, I had to seek out mentors to get answers, making several mistakes along the way.

Native Assets solves that problem while also teaching everything you need to know to not just survive but ***thrive*** *in this new blockchain-based society.*

"

– Sae'Von Springer

About Native Assets

Native Assets is a blockchain firm specializing in educational training, detailed industry analysis & corporate advising. Our mission? Empower you with the knowledge & insights to navigate + flourish in the new digital asset era - the *blockchain* era.

Blockchain Foundations

Ready to master blockchain & crypto investing? Check out "*Blockchain Foundations*", our 21-day seminar program.

One part education, one part mentorship, "*Blockchain Foundations*" is a university-level program anchored by action-oriented goals typical of private coaching programs. "*Foundations*" empowers you towards total mastery of digital asset investing through interdisciplinary study of blockchain technologies + cryptographic currencies, investing principles, trading techniques, passive income strategies, security + more - all contained within focused training modules. It is not the scope of topics covered but rather their coherent synthesis that provides valuable wisdom & actionable insights. After all, knowledge, ***applied***, is power.

To register visit **www.nativeassets.co/foundations**

Leave A Review

It's an honor to bring you this important information during such a pivotal time in society. The mission has always been to teach the community "how to fish" in this new blockchain era. If you enjoyed this book, found this information insightful, have grown & been enriched from any of our efforts at Native Assets, I humbly request that you leave a review on Amazon. By sharing a few words you'll be helping get this crucial work in front of a much wider audience who can use this information to grow & thrive in this changing world alongside us. I am immensely grateful for your generosity of time & thank you for doing your part in helping us realize a more equitable future where everyone, not just the select few, can enjoy an extraordinary life of freedom, abundance + bliss.

To submit your review, join our free newsletter, listen to our podcast & more, please visit **www.nativeassets.co/links** or scan the QR code below.

Made in the USA
Columbia, SC
04 October 2021